LOOKING AFTER YOUR DOG

JOHN AND MARY HOLMES

LOOKING AFTER YOUR DOG

training and care

ARCO PUBLISHING, INC. NEW YORK

Published by Arco Publishing, Inc.
219 Park Avenue South, New York, N.Y. 10003

© John and Mary Holmes 1981

First published in Great Britain in 1981
by Ward Lock Limited, 47 Marylebone Lane,
London W1M 6AX, a Pentos Company.

Library of Congress Cataloging in Publication Data

Holmes, John, 1913-
   Looking after your dog.

   1. Dogs. 2. Dogs—Training. I. Holmes, Mary.
II. Title.
SF427.H766 1981   636.7   81-4894
ISBN 0-668-05271-6 (pbk.)   AACR2

Printed in Singapore by Kyodo-Shing Loong Printing Industries Pte Ltd.

Contents

Introduction 7

1 Understanding the dog's instincts 9

2 The new puppy 21

3 Basic training 29

4 Obedience training 43

5 Applied training 58

6 General care 70

7 Health and first aid 78

8 Play and exercise 84

Useful addresses 91

Index 93

Introduction

The dog is a fascinating subject and many books have been written on the various aspects of dog behaviour and ownership. The more that is learnt about the dog, the more there is to be learnt.

Over the years, we have come in contact with many dogs and their owners, the majority of whom have problems of one sort or another. In our efforts to solve these problems we always come back to asking ourselves the basic question—where and why did the owner go wrong? Significantly, it is seldom that the owner can answer this question. Which brings us to the chief cause of dog problems—only a small minority of owners understand dogs, including their own dog. Far too much emphasis is put on what might be called the mechanics of training, and too little on understanding the dog's mind. For instance, we are told that a certain type of choke chain is essential for training dogs, but we are never told why it is so essential. A knowledge of why the dog wants to do some things but not others will often enable the owner to prevent bad habits that could later prove very difficult to cure.

Our own experience has convinced us that there are no rules that can be applied to all dogs or all owners. And we would ask the reader not to flip over the pages looking for the chapter on his particular problem, be it teaching a dog to walk on a lead, or whatever. Please read the book from beginning to end and try to understand what makes dogs 'tick'. Apply this knowledge in studying your own dog and find out what it is that makes him different from all other dogs.

To help you understand your dog has been one of our main aims in writing this book. If we have succeeded, we believe you will have much more pleasure from him. And, just as important, you will make life much more enjoyable for your dog.

1 Understanding the dog's instincts

There are many reasons for wanting to keep a dog, some good, some bad. However, whatever the reason, one important fact is all too often overlooked—those who accept the privilege of keeping a dog must also accept the responsibilities that go with it. Those who are unwilling to accept those responsibilities should not keep a dog. After all, no one is obliged to keep a dog—it is something that one accepts of one's own free will.

Firstly, there is the responsibility to the dog himself. Most people consider that they cover this by feeding, grooming and exercising. They overlook the fact that, to a dog just as much as to a human, mental exercise is no less important than physical. Trained dogs are invariably happier than untrained ones, and all dogs should have at least some elementary training.

Secondly, and no less important, is the responsibility to other members of the community. The vast numbers of stray dogs and the ever-increasing anti-dog movement are due entirely to the failure of dog owners either to accept that responsibility or to put it into practice.

We disagree with some of our contemporaries, who maintain that all dogs are good and it is only the owners who are bad. We meet many people who fully realize their responsibilities and try very, very hard to comply with them, and still end up with a dog that bites the postman, or themselves, causes a road accident, or does something else that is equally unacceptable. Why? Because so few dog owners understand canine mentality.

These people regard dogs as 'almost human', which is a great insult to our canine friends. The dog has become man's best friend, not because he is almost human, but because he can do so many things that we cannot do. And even in this scientific age, we still don't know how he does some of those things, such as detecting mines and drugs.

Many people regard intelligence as the most important factor in a dog's make-up and believe that the more intelligent a dog is, the easier he will be to train. In fact, nearly all problem dogs are very intelligent. The cat is quite as intelligent as the dog but he is not a very good training proposition!

Perhaps most important of all is the fact that few dog owners understand canine instincts and their importance to the man/dog relationship.

As a result of all this, many very responsible and well-meaning people buy a puppy of their chosen breed and spend the rest of his life trying to fit a square peg into a round hole. This causes great unhappiness to the dog, provides little pleasure (often great worry) to the owner and breaks many neighbourly friendships.

The association of ideas

Dogs, and indeed all animals, learn by association of ideas. Scientists tell us that they do not reason at all. They simply react to what is happening and do not think about what has happened or is about to happen. However, scientists usually work with animals under controlled conditions, often in laboratories. Most people like ourselves, who train and work dogs—and live with them too—believe that they do sometimes work out problems for themselves. All the same, it is very difficult to tell whether a dog has worked out how to do something or whether he just happened to do it by chance. It is, therefore, a great mistake to assume that a dog reasons. All training should be based on the assumption that the dog does not reason, and that he learns by association of ideas.

It is surprising how many people have difficulty in understanding the association of ideas, which applies to humans just as much as to other animals. We all associate certain sounds, sights or smells with certain experiences, and sometimes they bring back very vivid memories throughout our lives. And different people can, and often do, associate the same sound or sight with very different experiences. A certain tune may bring back very happy memories to one person and very sad or even terrifying memories to another. The same can apply to the sight of a boy with a telegram. All of us can think of some things which we associate with certain events every time we see or hear them.

Yet one meets people who say, 'I am afraid of Alsatians! You see I was bitten by one as a child'. Then they say, 'I cannot understand why our puppy was so fond of children when we got him and now he hates them'. We are then told a 'terribly funny story' of how, when the new puppy arrived, the baby of the house crawled up behind him and banged him on the head with his rattle!

The object of training is to build up the associations of ideas that will be to our advantage, and try to avoid those that are to our disadvantage. Before starting, there are certain very important points to remember. Firstly, the strongest and most

If a puppy has an unpleasant or frightening experience, such as being hit by a small child, it will make a deep impression on him. It will make him nervous in the future of the experience being repeated.

lasting associations are often allied to fear. There are people who cannot go near a certain place where they had a terrible fright. And there are those who cover their ears in an effort to shut out a sound which they associate with a terrifying experience. If we bear in mind that these people can reason and, in many cases, will try very hard for years to overcome their fear, it should be easy to understand just how much a bad fright can affect an animal.

Fortunately for us and our animals, enjoyable events also create very strong associations. Generally speaking, the more enjoyable the event, the more vividly it is remembered.

Another very important point to remember is that first associations, good or bad, are much stronger than subsequent ones. Most dog exhibitors are aware of the fact that, if a puppy gets a bad fright at his first show, he may be put off showing for life. However, if he has been to several shows and enjoys going to them and then gets frightened, it is unlikely to have anything like as lasting an effect.

For training purposes we try to create the associations we want and avoid those that we do not want, by what is known as correction and reward. In this connection, correction is something of a misnomer. It does not necessarily mean beating the dog or jerking him on a choke chain. It really means any act which forces the dog to obey—like pushing him into a sitting position. A dog can be rewarded in many different ways, depending on the individual animal and what he has done. Food is condemned by many dyed-in-the-wool 'obedience enthusiasts', but we use it regularly. Most dogs like to be fussed, petted and talked to in a friendly voice. Anything which the dog likes can be used as a reward.

Instincts

The end product, be it an enjoyable asset or an unpleasant liability, is not entirely dependent on correction and reward. The dog's natural instincts play a vital role. Indeed, it is almost certain that the main reason why man first domesticated the dog was because he had so many instincts which could be useful to him. It is, therefore, surprising that, when man has been using the dog for his own benefit for thousands of years, the average dog owner of today has not the haziest idea of the instincts inherent in the animal lying on the hearth beside him. There are few dog owners who can differentiate between instinct and intelligence. Instinct might be described as an urge from within which makes a dog act in a certain way. This is due as much to his inability to resist the action as to his desire to carry it out. It has no connection whatsoever with intelligence.

The first instinct to make itself apparent is the instinct for survival. Immediately he is born, the young puppy squirms about until he finds a teat and then sucks it. Neither intelligence nor learning by association of ideas play any part in this process; it is pure instinct that drives the puppy to find food.

Similarly, it is the maternal instinct that tells the female to clean up the foetal membrane and fluid and to stir the puppy into action by licking it. She does not have to be taught how to do it and she is unlikely to have seen another female doing it. Indeed, a maiden female is unlikely ever to have seen a newborn puppy before her own.

Canine instincts vary enormously in strength between different breeds, and individuals of the same breed. Again taking the maternal instinct as an example, we find that in some females it is so strong that they will happily adopt puppies belonging to other females, as well as kittens and many other orphaned babies. On the other hand some, which look after their own offspring very well will, if given the chance, kill newborn puppies belonging to another female. Some are so devoid of maternal instinct that they simply walk off and leave their puppies to die. Intelligence plays no part in their behaviour, and an exceptionally intelligent female can be really stupid when it comes to looking after a family. Likewise, many females of low intelligence make most efficient mothers.

Most instincts provide pleasure to the dog, and because it associates the action with pleasure the instinct grows stronger with usage. The maiden female will usually look with amazement at her first puppy, refusing to touch it for quite some time. As soon as she starts licking it she will become more and more enthusiastic, sometimes almost frantic, in her efforts to clean it. She will start licking her second puppy immediately, and when she has her next litter there will be no hesitation at all in cleaning the first puppy.

Another example of the dog's instinctive behaviour is a puppy retrieving a ball in response to the retrieving/hunting instinct, with which we shall be dealing more fully later on. Many puppies will run after a ball and pick it up, sometimes bringing it back and sometimes running off to play with it. The first time it sees the ball 'running away', the puppy will usually lollop after it only half seriously. If the game is continued, however, it will quickly become more and more enthusiastic until it can be relied upon to fetch a ball every time it is thrown. This is one instinct which can grow stronger with usage to the extent of becoming overdeveloped, and many dogs are obsessed by balls, sticks, stones or anything else they can carry.

There seems to be an age at which a dog's instincts tend to develop. A puppy which has shown no previous inclination to retrieve may suddenly decide to do so. If encouraged at this stage the instinct should quickly develop, but if discouraged it will almost certainly weaken and possibly die out altogether. A dog which has never been allowed to play with a ball as a puppy is very unlikely to do so as an adult. Whether or not instincts flourish depends to a great extent on the strength of the instinct in the first place. Some dogs, particularly the gun dog breeds, have very strong retrieving instincts which will survive under very adverse conditions. At the opposite extreme, other dogs are so completely devoid of the retrieving instinct that it is impossible to persuade them to pick up anything at all. In between are the majority of dogs, which require training to develop the retrieving instinct or to keep it under control, as the case may be.

Instinct is something which is either there or not there. It can be strengthened, weakened or diverted, but it cannot be put there and it cannot be taken away. It may lie dormant throughout a dog's life, but once developed it can never be weakened again. A dog with an obsession for chasing balls may be controlled by training and by providing other outlets for his energy, but the basic obsession will always remain. Likewise, if a young dog is severely corrected the first time he chases a car he may well give up the idea. But if allowed to chase cars, the hunting instinct will become stronger each time he does so and in a very short time it will be very difficult, even impossible, to cure the habit.

The most important canine instincts in a dog's relationship with man are the pack instinct, the instinct of self-preservation, the sex instinct, the hunting instinct, the guarding instinct, and the instinct to keep the nest clean (which will be dealt with in a later chapter).

We shall start with the pack instinct. All the higher animals have what is known as a 'pecking order', so called because it was first studied scientifically in poultry. A 'pecking order' simply means that in a flock of twenty-six birds, A can peck anyone from B–Z, B pecks anyone from C–Z, but not A; C pecks anyone from D–Z, but not A or B and so on, down to poor Z who can peck no one but is pecked by everyone. In dogs it is not nearly so simple, although at first sight the principle is very similar. The pack leader does not simply dominate his subordinates, he actually keeps them all in order and tells them what to do. When the leader says 'Let's go hunting', they all go hunting; and when he says 'It's time to go home', they all go home. The majority of pack leaders are males, but a female can, and quite often does, take on the role. Although every canine pack has a leader, the other members of the pack do not follow in a straightforward pecking order from B–Z. Often there are quite a number of dogs who neither dominate nor are dominated. Age also plays an important part and quite often one senior member of the pack will become more and more dominant until he attains the position of second-in-command. Very often, he will wait for an opportunity to overthrow the leader and take over that position for himself. If a pack leader dies without leaving a successor, there is considerable fighting and confusion until a new leader emerges to take control.

Large packs of dogs are normally only found in the wild, but, having kept quite a large and varied pack of domestic dogs ourselves for some thirty years, we have seen that this pack instinct is still very much alive in the domestic dog.

As already mentioned, dogs are not 'almost human' and great suffering can be caused to them by people who think they are. In fact, in some ways we are almost canine! Human and canine social habits have many similarities and it is this which enables man to take over the role of pack leader. The dog's willingness to accept a human master as a substitute for a canine pack leader makes him easier to train than most other animals. Not only is he willing to be trained, he actually wants to be trained, and owners who neglect this can cause just as much suffering as those who starve their dogs.

The instinct of self-preservation, which makes most wild dogs furtive and afraid of the unfamiliar, is one of the instincts which is of little or no benefit to man. It is from this instinct in the wild dog that nervousness in the domestic dog has evolved, and nervousness is one of the most common causes of problems in present-day dogs. Nearly all cases of children being attacked by dogs and people being bitten by their own dogs arise from nervousness; the dog is afraid it is going to be hurt and attacks first. In the evolution of the domestic dog, the instinct of self-preservation has been considerably weakened by simply breeding from bold dogs rather than nervous ones, but it has never been entirely removed.

Although it is essential if we are to continue breeding dogs, the sex instinct is another instinct which is of no benefit to man and, under present-day conditions, is rarely of any benefit to the dog himself. Indeed, far from providing any pleasure (some people still argue that it does) it is much more likely to turn the poor dog into a target for buckets of water, shot gun pellets and various other 'deterrents' frequently used by owners of females in season. Perhaps the saddest aspect of all this is that it is unnecessary. The sex instinct is the only instinct which can be removed by a simple surgical operation; castrating the male and spaying the female.

The castrated male is not only happier, free from the worry and frustration of local females, he is also a much pleasanter animal to have around. He should lose some of his pack-leader instinct, making him less likely to mark his territory by urinating on furniture, less likely to fight other males and more submissive to the wishes of his human pack leader. We have owned and trained castrated dogs for some thirty years now and have not found that it alters any of the other instincts at all. Dogs guard, hunt, work sheep and retrieve game just as well after castration as before.

It is most important that males should not be castrated before they have reached maturity, otherwise they lack character and initiative and become lazy, fat 'eunuchs'. The age at which a male reaches sexual maturity varies enormously between individuals. Generally speaking, small breeds mature more quickly than large ones. The first clear indication is when he starts 'lifting his leg', which may be as early as six months or as late as eighteen months. It is usually better to castrate too late than too early, and we have known dogs castrated at six or seven years old with no ill effects. It is better to leave a submissive male until he is older, while a dominant one should be operated on much sooner—usually when he starts being a nuisance!

There is some difference of opinion as to the best age to spay females, but it is usually advisable to leave them until they have come in season at least once. Unlike castration, spaying done at the right time does not change a female's character at all. The owner who does not want to breed is saved a great deal of trouble and worry, and the female is spared the ordeal of being confined for three weeks twice a year. There is also some evidence to suggest that spayed females may be healthier, with less uterine disorders and no risk of false pregnancies.

Of all the dog's instincts none has been more useful than the hunting instinct. There is little doubt that the first purpose for which man used the dog would be to help him catch his food. In other words the dog just did what it had always done in order to survive. And there is also little doubt that from earliest times man would breed from the best hunting dogs, destroying those which did not come up to scratch. The result is that, in many breeds of domestic dog, the hunting instinct is far stronger than in their wild ancestors. Unfortunately, this important fact is all too often overlooked.

Of course the human animal also has a strong hunting instinct, handed down from our ancestors. In few advanced societies does anyone have to hunt to live. However, many whose food comes out of cans still hunt in response to the hunting instinct. Some hunt animals which they have no intention of eating, while others, who claim to be animal lovers, hunt the hunters, and some form packs which mug helpless old ladies. All of which shows just how long an instinct can survive

It is the wild dog's instinct to stalk his prey that makes a Border Collie (*right*) 'eye' a sheep, or a Pointer (*below*) 'point' a bird.

without any real use for it. This applies much more to the dog, which has been bred specifically to hunt in order to help man follow his own hunting instinct.

The hunting instinct has been modified—again by careful selective breeding—to produce the herding instinct in sheepdogs. Few people seem to realize that the sheepdog 'eyeing' a sheep or the bird dog setting a partridge are responding to exactly the same instinct—an instinct derived from the wild dog's instinct to hunt its prey.

The unfortunate aspect of all this is that what was the dog's greatest asset 100 years ago, or even less, is his greatest liability today. Nearly all cases of sheep or poultry worrying, car or bicycle chasing, and often of biting children who are playing, is the direct result of a frustrated hunting instinct.

Instincts can be strengthened or weakened by training and by the opportunity or lack of opportunity to use them. They also can be and have been strengthened or weakened by careful selective breeding. Through the ages, man has bred dogs to suit his own purposes, and in the process different breeds have evolved with their own characteristics. For many, but not all, of man's purposes, the submissive aspect of the pack instinct is

more important than the dominant aspect. We find breeds where the majority are submissive and willing to learn, while in others the majority are dominant and anxious to lead rather than be led.

A Greyhound chases a hare in response to the same instinct as a sheepdog works sheep. But as a result of selective breeding, various breeds of sheepdog have emerged where the majority are willing, even anxious to be trained. The same applies to gun dogs. With Greyhounds, Afghan Hounds and other hunting breeds the picture is a very different one. Once a hound has been unleashed to pursue his quarry, his master ceases to play any part. In many cases he simply follows it, so that in fact we have the dog leading and the master following. It is obvious that, for this type of work, a strong submissive instinct is not required, and hounds (and terriers too) are therefore generally much more difficult to train than gundogs and sheepdogs. This is not due to lack of intelligence, and of course many hounds and terriers can be and are trained to be obedient, well-behaved animals. Hounds in particular become completely different animals when away from any quarry and will happily curl up on the best settee as though they wouldn't harm a fly.

Whether or not a dominant breed can be trained raises an aspect of the pack instinct which is often overlooked. It is easy for man to take over as pack leader to his dog or dogs, but only if he is capable of leading. Nearly anyone can train a submissive dog, but a dominant dog can only be trained by a dominant person. Within a household, it is common to find that the dog will obey some members of the family but not others.

In recent years, trainers have tried more and more to study and practise the methods used by the canine pack leaders, with very successful results.

A good pack leader commands respect without bullying. He (or she) does not need to keep proving how big and strong he is, and therefore, does not put himself in a position to be challenged. The most important lesson for the human owner to learn from the canine pack leader is that, by gaining the respect of his subordinates, he will also gain their affection and loyalty. The bully who rules by force may obtain implicit obedience, but at the loss of friendship or affection.

Unfortunately, a large number of trainers (including very successful trainers in trials and competitions of various types) adopt the latter policy. Never having trained by any other method, they have no idea of the pleasure they are losing in not having a dog which is a faithful companion and partner.

Many breeders put forward the argument that all dogs are good and that the bad ones have been ruined by their owners, as an excuse for the untrainable puppies they have sold. Probably, the end product depends about 50 per cent on inherited characteristics and 50 per cent on acquired ones. Bearing in mind that the new dog will, hopefully, be a member of the family for the next ten to fifteen years, most people go to far too little trouble *before* they buy one.

Choosing the right dog

There is no shortage of dogs. Dog homes all over the world are full of them and thousands are put down every day. But there *is* a shortage of good dogs. While many of those in dog homes are just unfortunate, many more are there because they got into trouble of one sort or another. An adult dog is just as likely to become attached to a new owner as one acquired as a puppy. But, before taking one on, find out why he wants a new home. Most people start with a puppy for two reasons. Firstly, there are many more puppies available to choose from. Secondly, immense pleasure can be derived from rearing a puppy from scratch.

Temperament is by far the most important factor in choosing a puppy. In dogs, a good temperament is one that is bold, friendly and not afraid of noise or people; a bad temperament is one that is shy or nervous in any way. The majority of puppies may appear to have good temperaments, but only a minority end up as bold, friendly dogs. In choosing a puppy, his own behaviour is less important than the behaviour of his parents, grandparents and even great-grandparents. It is unlikely that you will be able to see all of these, but do try to see the parents and as many relatives as possible. If they are not the sort of dogs you would like to own, try somewhere else.

You should pay particular attention to the temperament of the dam. Geneticists believe that an animal inherits its various characteristics 50/50 from sire and dam. By the time he is weaned, a puppy will also have acquired other characteristics from his mother, or foster mother, as the case may be. Experiments have been carried out where puppies from a bold mother have been fostered onto a shy one, and vice versa. These have shown quite conclusively that fear of any sort, and gun shyness in particular, is transmitted to the puppies by the time they are three or four weeks old.

Recent study has shown that in the first few weeks of their lives, puppies learn much more than was previously believed. This has nothing to do with training, but simply with the conditions surrounding the puppy in his early life. By the time the puppy is eight weeks old, his instinct to keep his 'nest' clean can either be well developed or completely killed. Socialization with human beings should be developed from the time the puppy's eyes are open. At one time it was considered bad for puppies to be petted and handled by children, but a puppy that is used to being handled from an early age will settle into his new home much more quickly. Provided that he goes to the right home, the sooner the puppy leaves his brothers and sisters, the better. The best age is usually between seven and eight weeks old.

Supposing that you have found a litter of puppies of your chosen breed, that you like the parents and that the pups have been well reared under reasonable conditions, what should you look for in the puppy himself? First of all remember that, although the puppies may look very much alike now, they will all grow up with very different characters, just like any family of brothers and sisters. And if you have just lost one of the same breed, don't expect any of these puppies to grow up just like your previous dog.

In nearly every litter there is a dominant puppy, which is quicker to learn than the others—very often learning how to escape! It is usually, but not invariably, a male and as soon as the pups can crawl he will be first out of the nest, first to the feed bowl and almost certainly first to greet you on arrival. In later life this puppy will probably be a good worker, but he will also often be very dominant and wilful, and therefore difficult to train. The second, or even third puppy in the social scale is often a better choice, but much depends on the parents. If the parents are hard dogs, choose the most submissive puppy, but if they are very amenable, soft dogs then you want to go for a bold puppy, even the number one puppy. And don't forget to consider whether you are a dominant or submissive person.

Take plenty of time looking at a litter of pups and discussing them with the breeder, who knows, or should know, each puppy individually. The puppy to choose is the one which comes to you when you squat down to speak to him, which snuggles up to you when you take him in your arms, and which does not run away if you clap your hands or make an unexpected movement. The puppy you should leave behind is the independent one which stalks off, minding his own business, which struggles to get out of your arms when you pick him up or which runs away when you clap your hands. And the puppy you should not have on any account is the one which, on seeing a stranger, runs into his kennel or hides in a corner. Many people feel sorry for the shy puppy and buy him, only to regret having done so for the rest of the dog's life. It is also very cruel to keep a nervous dog in a house full of rowdy children, or under any other noisy conditions. To force an animal to live in constant fear of everything around him is very cruel.

Always look for a dog with a bright, bold eye, which looks

straight at you honestly, and avoid any dog with a shifty, furtive look. Bright eyes are a guide to physical well-being as well as temperament, and it is equally important to start with a healthy puppy. His skin should be soft and pliable when picked up in the hand and his coat should be glossy, although some types of coat do not look glossy even when in the best condition. The skin should be free from sores and bare patches, which can be due to fleas or lice, usually easily cured, but sometimes caused by a type of mange which may be impossible to cure. If the puppy is pot bellied, it is probably due to worms, which are easy to treat, but it is a sign of neglect, or ignorance, on the part of the breeder as the pup should have been wormed before this stage.

2 The new puppy

Once you have taken the decision to have a puppy, remember that the beginning of it all is *not* when you fetch the pup home, but *before* you do so. No mother-to-be would think of going off to hospital to have her baby without having left everything ready at home. But many well-meaning people bring a puppy home completely forgetting they have not bought any puppy food, they have no bed for the wee mite and suddenly realizing it's the weekend and the shops are shut!

Preparation and arrival

Let's take a look at what will be needed for the pup's safety, comfort, and future well being. A warm, draught-proof bed is a must. There are numerous excellent designs of dog beds on the market, which will be discussed later. Until the pup has stopped growing—and chewing—a cardboard box will suit him fine. All puppies chew and a mouthful of cardboard will do him far less harm than bits of plastic or sharp pieces chewed out of a basket. Put the box on its side so that it makes an enclosed bed in which the pup will feel more secure. Bedding needs to be washable as well as warm. An old blanket or towel will do, but the simulated fur blankets especially made for dogs are excellent. They reflect body heat, and any damp soaks through and can be absorbed by newspaper underneath, keeping the blanket dry. They are difficult to chew and very easy to wash.

Decide where you are going to put the bed. The kitchen or utility room are sensible choices. These generally have washable floors, are warm but not hot and stuffy and often have a back door out to the yard or garden. The latter can prove very useful when a quick exit is needed! A playpen to go round the bed is very useful, although not a necessity. This can be bought from most pet shops. Put the playpen in the corner of whichever room you have decided on as the puppy's sleeping place. Puppies, like babies, need plenty of sleep and very soon the pup will learn that this is his own place where he can rest, sleep or play in safety. It will keep him out of mischief, stop him puddling all over the house, you will know where he is when

A playpen is very useful for a young puppy. At this stage a cardboard box on its side is suitable for a bed, which should have a piece of blanket or something similar for the pup to lie on—not a cushion. The rest of the floor should be covered with newspaper. Fresh water should always be available. Any rubber toys should be of good quality so that the puppy cannot break off little pieces and swallow them.

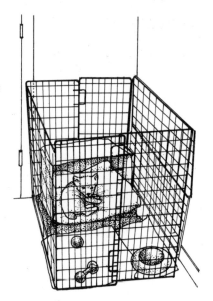

you are too busy to watch him, and it will generally make life much easier for the puppy and the whole family.

A puppy of a very small breed like a Chihuahua is probably better off in an indoor kennel or travelling box; some of these 'tinies' feel cold and lost in a large open playpen. A travelling box has the advantage that, when the puppy is older, it can be used as a portable kennel—if you are travelling away from home or going to a dog show, for instance. Some breeds, such as smooth Dachshunds, feel the cold more than others, and for any of these a small heated electric pad is useful. These are shockproof and chewproof, and slipped under the blanket they maintain a constant, very low heat.

Two feed bowls will be necessary, one for food and one for water. These must be kept clean; dirty food bowls are a common cause of diarrhoea. Aluminium or stainless steel are good, but earthenware is even better as it is almost impossible to tip up. Plastic bowls are not very sensible for puppies. They are very light, easily knocked over and invariably get chewed.

Few puppies need much grooming, but it is a good idea to get them used to it before it becomes a necessity—especially if they are likely to grow into large hairy monsters! A brush and comb is likely to be all that is needed, but ask the breeder's advice about grooming before you collect the puppy.

If you bring the puppy home when he is about eight weeks old, which is quite usual, you will not, or should not, be taking him for walks for some weeks. But now is the time to get him used to wearing a collar and once he is used to that he can be accustomed to walking on a lead, even if it is in his own back yard. A soft leather collar is best and at the same time buy a dog tag with your name, address and telephone number engraved on it. This is a legal necessity in many countries. Don't have the plate on the collar engraved. The pup will soon grow out of his collar and need a larger one. If you have a dog tag this can be removed and replaced on the new collar. Buy a long, light lead in either leather or nylon.

Like most young animals, puppies love toys. Rawhide chew sticks in various shapes, such as bones or slippers, are usually popular and good for the teeth. Good quality rubber bones or balls, hard enough not to be chewed up, and large enough not to be swallowed, are also good. Resist the temptation to give the pup an old slipper. It will only encourage him to think all slippers are for playing with and if he chews it up he will get more than a slight tummy ache!

All reputable breeders will supply a diet sheet and whatever ideas you might have about feeding, stick to this for the first week or so. It is a very traumatic experience for a small puppy to go to his first home, so don't add to the stress by suddenly changing his diet. He will probably be having four meals a day and as you will, obviously, want to have him house clean as soon as you can, don't feed him too late at night. These meals should gradually be reduced in number to one or at the most two by the time the dog is twelve months old. A growing puppy will need considerably more good quality food in proportion to his size than an adult dog. First-time owners are very apt to overfeed little breeds and underfeed large ones. If you decide to alter the diet do so gradually. There are a number of specially prepared commercial puppy foods available so if you find one that suits your pocket and on which the puppy thrives stick to it. But if you have small children in the family the puppy will do very well with the same baby cereals that the kids have, for some of his meals.

That covers most of the items you will need to start with, but there are a few other things you should see to. Check the garden or yard. Very small puppies seem able to wriggle out of even smaller gaps in the fence. And all puppies can enlarge very, very small gaps at an alarming speed! So make at least a small part of the garden 'puppyproof'.

Find out the name, address and telephone number of a good small animal veterinary surgeon. Go to see him and have a chat about the puppy you are going to have. The pup should have been wormed before you buy him, but he will certainly want worming again. He may also have had some of the necessary vaccinations. Today most dogs are vaccinated against distemper, hepatitis and leptospirosis and, more recently, parvo virus. In some countries a rabies vaccination is also compulsory. So it is important to sort all this out with your

veterinary surgeon before the puppy arrives. Make an appoint-
ment for the vaccinations needed and, if you want to remain
friends with your veterinary surgeon, don't forget it! With the
ever-rising costs of veterinary attention a reputable pet
insurance policy could be a good investment. There are several
schemes, most of which cover the cost of drugs and treatment
up to a certain sum. For a small additional fee, cover can be
arranged for third party claims should the dog bite anyone or
cause an accident.

The most important point to remember with a young puppy
is that he is still a baby. It is surprising how many people
overlook this fact. They have some idea that if they don't start
training their puppy right away, he can never be trained. At this
age, however, the puppy does not need a replacement pack
leader so much as a replacement mother. There is no such thing
as giving a puppy too much affection, but don't forget that, like
all babies, he needs plenty of sleep. Much suffering is caused to
puppies that go to new homes where children are allowed to
maul and play with them continuously.

New owners often make the mistake of starting to house train
the puppy the moment they get him home. They take this
infant from his brothers and sisters and familiar surroundings, probably on a long car journey, then put him down on the
kitchen floor, whereupon he does what any sensible person
would expect him to do. And the owner immediately smacks
him for leaving a puddle on the floor. But, as already said,
animals do not reason as we do, they learn by association of
ideas. Rather than associating the punishment with the 'crime',
as the owner intended, the puppy is more likely to associate the
punishment with the person who administered it and with his
new home in general. This kind of treatment turns many bold,
friendly puppies into timid, nervous wrecks within a few days
of going to a new home. It seems surprising that mothers will
wrap their own children in nappies, yet expect a canine infant to
go through the night without relieving himself.

Correction and reward: the behaviour of the mother

The best way to learn how to take over from the puppy's
mother is to study her behaviour. She is constantly licking and
caressing her puppies and pushing them about in play. This is
not to suggest that you start licking your new charge, but a
tense or worried puppy will often relax immediately in response
to the touch of a sensitive and sympathetic hand. The mother
also 'talks' to her puppies in very soft tones, usually inaudible to
human ears, so try to talk to your puppy in a quiet, reassuring

tone of voice. This does not mean subjecting him to a barrage of meaningless chatter; talk to him when there is a reason for doing so and try to get some response.

If a puppy annoys his mother, say by biting too hard in play, she will growl at him and, if that has no effect, snap at him. Next time she growls at the puppy, he will associate the sound with correction and stop whatever he is doing. A sudden snap from the mother is reserved for more serious misbehaviour. It nearly always frightens the puppy, and he will almost certainly draw back and may even run away. But very soon he will come back and probably roll on his back in front of mum. Her response to this is to lick and caress the puppy, making friendly noises and reassuring him in every way she can that she still loves him—*so long as he behaves himself*.

The human 'mother' can, and should, learn several things from this behaviour. The female corrects the puppy as and when he is doing the wrong thing; not several seconds or even minutes after, as so many humans do. And once the puppy has been corrected, it is over and all is forgiven. Very soon the puppy associates a growl with correction and will stop whatever he is doing. A puppy reacts instinctively to a growl and it is very seldom that a puppy will go right up to a strange dog that growls at him. This instinct can be, and should be, used in training.

To give a practical example of how this treatment should work with your puppy, imagine he is chewing the hearth rug. You should say 'no' to him in a harsh growling tone (never shout—the puppy has better hearing than you). A sensitive puppy will probably react to this growl and stop chewing, whereupon you should praise him by stroking and encouraging him in a friendly tone. If he does not respond to the growl, follow immediately with correction, which, for a puppy of this age, can be a light tap on the nose or gripping the scruff of his neck. As soon as the puppy responds, praise him well. A lively puppy will probably take some time to learn, but repeat the whole performance more severely each time until he gives up.

Learning his name

It is important to remember that 'No' is not the first sound a puppy should learn to understand. Dogs do not understand words, only sounds. It is just as easy to teach a dog to lie down by saying 'stand up' as it is by saying 'lie down'. The first sound a new puppy should learn is his name. He should learn to associate his name with pleasure and your first objective should be to get him to come to you every time he hears the sound of his name.

One of the most common of all dog problems is that dogs will not come when they are called. Most of these dogs have been taught not to come, because the owner has created the wrong associations. Some have been taught to run away by the owner's efforts to train them. For a young puppy in a new home, every effort should, therefore, be made to make him associate his name with pleasure. Later on, the name can be used in different tones, but for the present it must always be spoken in a friendly, reassuring tone. Never shout the puppy's name and never use his name to scold him. Use a harsh 'no' or 'ahh', which can be growled rather than spoken. Don't keep repeating the puppy's name. That will simply accustom him to a sound which he will learn to ignore, like the radio or conversation. And don't call him when there is no chance whatsoever of him responding—for instance, when he is digging a hole in the garden or sees a dog in the distance. Call him when he happens to be coming in your direction of his own accord. When he reaches you, praise him enthusiastically and offer him some food. Next time the puppy hears his name, he should show more inclination to come towards you. The more you shout a puppy's name without getting any response, the more you are teaching him not to come when called.

House training

The first thing most people want to teach a puppy is to be house clean. To the majority of owners it is much more important that the puppy should be clean in the house than that he should be happy. What they overlook is the fact that a happy puppy is more likely to be clean than an unhappy one. There are two important points to remember here. Firstly, we are dealing with a baby; and secondly, unlike some other babies, the puppy has a natural instinct to keep his living quarters clean. Babies cannot go for any length of time without emptying both bladder and bowels, and an instinct cannot develop if given no opportunity to do so. In other words, if the puppy cannot relieve himself out of doors, nature will force him to relieve himself indoors. And once this becomes a habit, it is very difficult to break.

The first few days in a puppy's new home are vital for teaching good habits. Vigilance and time spent in the early days will be more than repaid later on. You should notice when the puppy feels uncomfortable, although a young puppy may give very little warning. Pick him up gently and quietly and take him out. Don't *put* him out. *Take* him out and stay with him until he does what you want him to do, then praise him and bring him indoors again.

Puppies nearly always want to relieve themselves when they

wake up and after they have had a meal. So take yours out at these times, whether or not he shows any desire to do so. A puppy that has been brought up under clean conditions will soon go towards the door when he feels uncomfortable. All you have to do then is open the door. But remember that the puppy cannot open the door himself, and he cannot wait until you come back from shopping or finish a long telephone conversation. To punish a puppy who makes a mistake under these circumstances is pointless and cruel.

Few people have the time to keep a constant eye on a puppy. The answer to this is a playpen, which has already been mentioned. The pen should be placed as near as possible to the door, with a bed in one corner, and the floor should be covered with newspaper. There might appear to be a disadvantage in that the puppy will get into the habit of using the newspaper in his pen and will not want to go outside. But when the puppy is outside his pen, he will tend to go towards the pen if he wants to relieve himself. This should be obvious to you and you can easily put him outside—hence the reason for the pen being near the door. When eventually you remove the playpen and the newspaper altogether, the puppy should still head for the same spot and you can then open the door so that he can go straight into the yard or garden.

So far we have been dealing with the puppy brought up under good conditions, but not all puppies are brought up under good conditions. If the instinct to be clean is not strong enough in itself, something more drastic is necessary in an effort to develop it. You will need to teach the puppy what to do and what not to do by correction and reward. If the puppy just squats down wherever he happens to be without any warning, pick him up quickly, 'growl' with a 'no' and take him outside. Don't smack him, but don't be as gentle as you would be with a puppy which is trying to be clean. Being picked up firmly and quickly is a severe enough correction for a young puppy. A reasonably sensitive puppy will now associate feeling uncomfortable with correction, and this will worry him and make him hesitate the next time. Now is your opportunity to pick him up gently, talking to him in reassuring tones. This will help him to understand that he is doing the right thing, and also that you are still a nice person even if you did have to correct him for doing wrong. With a less sensitive puppy, you may have to repeat the correction several times before he gets the message and you may have to be more severe, even to the extent of grabbing him by the scruff of his neck and giving him a good shake. But *don't slap the puppy* and *don't correct him if you go into a room and find a puddle on the floor.* Just wipe the mess up and wait for an opportunity to catch the puppy in the act.

Whilst house training your puppy, apart from praising him when he relieves himself outside, take the opportunity to teach him a word of command. This way he will come to associate the word with the action, which helps in several ways. It can save you hanging around in the garden on a wet and windy night, and can be very useful when the pup is away from home.

Some puppies, taught to relieve themselves in a certain part of their own garden, are very reluctant to do likewise in a strange place. If you have taught him that when you say 'hurry up' (or whatever word or phrase you use) you want him to empty his bowels and/or bladder, he is far more likely to feel happy about doing so in a different place.

Most towns and cities are now full of notices telling you how much you will be fined if your dog fouls the pavement. But accidents can, and do, happen. Always make sure the dog has been out at home before you take him for a walk, especially in urban areas. If the worst does happen, don't drag the poor brute into the gutter to be terrified by the first passing car. Just quietly wait for him to finish. Keep a supply of strong plastic bags with you, take one out, slip your hand inside and scoop up the offending material. Catch the bag by the open end and pull it off, inside out. Put a twist round the top and drop it in the nearest litter bin. This way you will leave the pavement clean, the pup unworried and you will avoid a fine. But on such occasions never praise him—you certainly don't want to encourage him to squat in the middle of the pavement!

3 Basic training

Going on a leash

There is no great hurry to teach a puppy to go on a leash. He will learn just as easily at six months as six weeks—but if he is of a big breed and you are a small person the sooner you start the better. And it is important to get him out into the big wide world as soon as possible. As there are many occasions when it is essential to have a puppy on a leash, it is usually a good idea to accustom him to it quite early.

The first rule to be observed is never to put a puppy on a leash until he will follow you without one. The object of the leash is not to make the puppy stay with you but merely to prevent him straying away. He should stay with you and follow you about because he wants to—even if it is only in anticipation of the titbit you have in your hand!

There is some difference of opinion as to the best type of collar to use and there are people who would have us believe that collars train dogs. A collar, any collar, is merely a device which enables the trainer to physically restrain the dog and/or apply correction. It is a means of communication which helps the handler to train the dog. Most important of all, the collar which suits one dog may be quite unsuitable for another. The various types of collar for adult dogs are illustrated on page 43, but for the young puppy now under discussion the most suitable collar is the old fashioned leather one with buckle.

Earlier on, we advised you to put a collar on the puppy and allow him to become accustomed to it. Some puppies pay little or no attention, while others make frantic efforts to remove the horrid thing. In some cases the puppy may refuse to eat, in which case the collar should be removed at feeding times and afterwards replaced.

Once the puppy has accepted the collar and pays no attention to it the leash can be attached. This should be about $1\frac{1}{2}$ m (5 ft) long and of a strength appropriate to the dog. Nylon has, to a great extent, superseded leather for collars and leads and, in many ways, is better. Weight for weight, it is stronger than leather and remains pliable after getting wet. Unless leather is

Never drag a puppy to you on a leash. Use the leash to prevent him running away *(left)* and encourage him to come to you of his own accord *(right)*.

very well looked after (a rare occurrence) it becomes dry and brittle, eventually breaking.

All training should be carried out in a place familiar to the dog and as free as possible from distractions. Start the puppy on a leash in the garden or even the house. The first object is to let him realize that when the leash is on there is no way of escape, no matter how hard he tries. It is not really necessary to get him to go anywhere—just stand still. Few puppies want to stand still for long and he will soon discover that he can't go anywhere. This discovery brings forth a variety of reactions, from the puppy that panics to the one that sits down and sulks. As soon as the puppy has accepted the fact that he cannot get away, coax him to come to you, rewarding him with food when he does. Make the whole thing a game, never using the leash to make the puppy come to you, only to prevent him going away. Soon (sometimes right away) the puppy should be trotting round the garden after you, and he can then be taken out to new places.

Few people have much trouble persuading a puppy to go on a leash. It is when he is happy on the leash that the trouble starts—when he pulls. Unless checked almost before it starts, this will quickly become a habit and is one of the commonest problems with which professional trainers have to cope. The simple answer is—if the puppy pulls don't pull against him—jerk him back. If you do that the first time and *every* time he pulls, he should soon give up the idea. But dogs like pulling and are stronger than horses in proportion to their size. If allowed to pull, their necks become insensitive and they develop muscles to enable them to pull all the better. Their efficiency in this direction can be improved by using harness or spring-loaded leads. Once it has become a habit, severe corrective training is often necessary to stop a dog pulling and that will be discussed in a later chapter.

Car training

Most dog owners want to take their dogs with them in the car. Those who don't or won't miss half the pleasure to be derived from dog ownership. But considering the behaviour of some dogs one sees in cars, it is not surprising that so many people leave them at home!

There is no doubt at all that the earlier a puppy starts travelling, the more likely he is to accept and enjoy it. As already mentioned, a young puppy is less sensitive to his surroundings and therefore less likely to be car sick. He will also be smaller and therefore easier to control physically. And if he is sick, there won't be so much to clear up!

It is much better from the puppy's point of view, and safer too, to start off with two people, one to drive and one to look after the puppy. A small puppy is better sitting on the passenger's lap (protected by newspaper or towel), but a larger one will have to sit in the back. Don't allow him to scrabble about all over the car—and you! Make him stay still but don't be too hard on him if he is a bit miserable. Try to use a little common sense by not feeding the pup just before putting him in the car, and see that he has relieved himself too. If you think it unnecessary to mention such obvious points we can assure you that to many puppy owners they are not obvious at all. Some people will even argue that the pup must have his breakfast or he will be hungry. But if he eats a meal and then brings it up he will be just as hungry as if he had not been fed!

Don't get the idea that teaching a puppy to go in a car is inevitably a messy affair. Many puppies are never sick at all but, unfortunately, many are to begin with. And, unfortunately for them, many are denied for ever the pleasure of travelling with their owners. The owner takes the puppy out once (probably just after a meal) and it is sick. So they say 'Let's leave him until he's a bit older and he might be better'. He won't be better, but almost certainly worse. And the older he becomes the more upset he is likely to be.

Our own dogs must travel by car, sometimes very long distances, and we want them to arrive at the studio, or wherever, happy and enthusiastic. Over the years, we have started hundreds of puppies (and older dogs too) travelling by car. The only answer we have found is to start them as young as possible and take them out every day, if possible several times a day. Make the journeys short and with a happy ending. Drive the pup to the park or sea shore and let him out to enjoy himself. Soon he will associate the car with pleasure and want to go in it, in contrast to the pup which only goes in the car when he is being taken to the vet.

We have had many dogs which would start salivating and look miserable after a few miles. If possible we stop and take the dog out for a walk (the grass verge is better than nothing) and continue the journey without any further trouble. Some dogs that travel perfectly well in one car will immediately be sick in another, and many bad car travellers will travel perfectly well by rail, sea or air.

Sedatives and tranquillizers can be a great help in the early stages of travelling, but don't give the pup what you take yourself! Take him to your vet, who will prescribe something appropriate for his age and size. And don't turn him into a drug addict. As soon as there is some improvement gradually reduce the dose until it is no longer necessary.

We have had many dogs that were bad travellers—some very bad!—but we have never had one which did not get over it in the end. So persevere and keep taking your puppy with you.

Car sickness is by no means the only problem concerning travelling. Every day one sees dogs which obviously enjoy travelling and demonstrate their pleasure by leaping round and round the car barking at everything they see. Some people attempt to cope with the situation by dividing the car off with a dog guard. This merely restricts the area the dog has to charge around in and, although it may provide some safety for the driver, it does nothing to cure the problem.

This very obnoxious and common habit should be nipped in the bud. Habits can be compared to plants that, if trampled on as seedlings, can be severely retarded or killed altogether. But as they develop they become more and more resilient until the stage is reached where they are virtually impossible to eradicate. So if your dog shows the slightest inclination to do this, make a real effort to stop him before it becomes a habit. Get someone to drive you and have the dog on a chain slip collar with leash attached. If he shows the very slightest inclination to bark at anything try to jerk his head off (you won't succeed!) at the same time uttering a harsh 'no' or whatever comes naturally. If he responds, but not unless he responds, praise him well. The mistake so many people make in this sort of situation is to praise the dog for doing the wrong thing. Not intentionally, of course, but nevertheless efficiently. They coo and wheedle at the dog, 'It's all right; don't get excited; just calm down', and so on. During which time the dog continues to bark and is being encouraged by the tone of voice, and often by stroking too. Dogs do not understand words, only sounds and the tone in which they are uttered. A sharp jerk on the collar to stop the dog barking and *then* praise when he *has* stopped is what is necessary. In fact, exactly the same tactics as the mother employs when her puppy annoys her.

Being left alone

Almost as bad as the dog which barks when travelling is the one which barks incessantly when left in a parked car. Once again, the first essential is to prevent this from becoming a habit. Here, unfortunately, you will have to contend with the great dog-loving public, who will prove beyond any doubt that dogs are more intelligent than people! There are those who will tap on the window 'just to make friends'. Others will hold up their own little darling to have a look at the doggy in the car. And there are those who, when a dog barks, cannot resist 'barking' back at it. In an effort to avoid such people, always try to park in as quiet a place as possible. For instance, there is always much more to-ing and fro-ing in the middle of a car park than round the outside. With a small dog it is often a good idea to leave him in a travelling box where he cannot see what is going on and, more important, where passers-by cannot see him.

If you have a dog which has started barking when left alone, either in a car or in the house, you should set about correcting him as soon as you can. Leave him in the car but don't lock the doors and move the shortest distance that will enable you to be out of his sight. Wait until he starts barking and, when he is well tuned up, go back quickly and quietly, taking care that he does not see you approach—by no means easy with some dogs. Now open the car door quickly, grab hold of him by the scruff and shake him until his teeth rattle. By now he should have stopped barking so be nice to him, let him settle down and repeat the process until you get some response.

If you are in a public place, keep an eye open for dog lovers, who are liable to be far more vicious than any dog! You can beat the daylight out of a child or raise great weals on a horse without a word of protest. But raise a hand to a dog—that's different! The sad part about it is that dogs belonging to these people very often become such problems that they end up being destroyed.

It is easier to cope with the dog which barks when left alone in the house, or better still in a room in the house. In this case the dog is unable to see you approach, although he may well hear you. You must, therefore, shut the door and let him hear you walk away. Then wait until he is making a good old din. The more noise he is making the less likely he is to hear you returning and you can then treat him exactly as described in the car—and there are unlikely to be any onlookers!

The most important point to remember here is that it is the dog's mind you must try to work on, not his body. And remember what we said about frightening experiences creating the strongest associations of ideas. The average dog will be very frightened if someone suddenly opens the door and rushes at him. This will have far more effect than hundreds of gentle reprimands. But, and this is most important, it will only have the desired effect if the dog associates it with the crime. It is therefore absolutely vital that the dog is actually barking when you 'attack' him. If he stops barking as you approach, stop and stand still until he starts again. If he obviously realizes you are there, forget about it for the time being and wait for another opportunity.

Tying up

All dogs should learn to be tied up on a chain—at home. There is really no training to it. All that is necessary is to let the dog find out that, when he is tied up, he cannot escape. And also, that if he starts to bark he will be severely corrected as advised for the dog which barks in the house or car.

There are several very important points which should be borne in mind. It is always advisable to use a chain to start with. Obviously a dog cannot bite through a chain as it can with a rope or leash. It is also less likely to get wound round a leg, or legs. This is because a chain lies on the ground, and it does not kink like a leash does. The links should be fairly big—not the watch chain type.

Most important of all, the chain must have a swivel that swivels! All dog chains have swivels, but many don't work, either because of faulty construction or because they have been allowed to become rusty. If the dog is going to be left on the chain for any length of time, it is best to have two swivels, one at each end.

Amongst dog lovers there is often an aversion to leaving a dog chained up, probably due to the fact that so many savage dogs are seen tied up on short chains. But life is made up of alternatives, and before we decry anything we must consider what the alternatives are. Very few people are able to have their dog always with them, so what can they do with it? Many people shut it in the house and are proud to relate that he can last for twelve to sixteen hours without making a 'mistake'. This is not only downright cruelty, it is also the cause of much suffering from bladder and kidney trouble in older dogs.

Some people leave the dog in the garden, which is fine if the dog cannot escape. But many do escape, often causing road accidents that result in great suffering or death to themselves and human victims alike. And if they don't, they will certainly add to the innumerable problems caused by stray dogs. But to be secure for some dogs, a garden would resemble a prison and few people want to turn their gardens into prisons.

Most dogs will be just as happy on a long chain (or a short one on a running wire) as they will running around loose in a garden. They will do the garden far less harm too, and be much happier and healthier than shut up in a house. Of course, there should be a dog kennel with a comfortable bed. And there are other precautions you must also take. If the dog is on a running wire, see that the chain runs. The wire should be taut and if it is between two trees or posts see that there are stops far enough from the end to ensure that the dog cannot wind himself round the tree or post. Never tie a dog up on a single action slip collar. A buckled leather collar is usually best, but if the dog learns to slip this (many dogs do) a properly fitting double action slip collar will prevent his doing so. Most important of all, make quite sure that the chain is not long enough to allow the dog to jump a wall or fence and too short to allow him to land on the other side. Many dogs have been hanged in this way.

Even if there is no need to leave your dog chained up, there may be many occasions when it is very helpful to have a dog that can be tied up without worrying about it. A dog tied to the car bumper while you have a picnic can either enjoy the sun or lie in the shade of the car. Better for the dog than cooking in the car, and better for you than his disappearing into the distance.

Many shops nowadays have hitching rails to which dogs can be tied. And if dogs did not have more sense than the designers of these gadgets and the owners who tie dogs to them, there would be many serious accidents. One sees dogs, often strangers to each other, tied up so that they can tangle up each others leashes. And dogs are tied on such long leashes that they can cross the pavement and trip up any passer-by in the process. It is difficult to understand why so many people take dogs shopping, as few dogs seem to enjoy it. It is much better to get the shopping done and then take the dog for a decent run.

A dog tied on a running wire. Note the stop on the wire preventing the dog winding the chain round the post.

Dogs make very good protectors of young children, but should never be tied to a pram or push chair.

Another sight one frequently sees in towns is a dog, often quite a big dog, tied to a pram. The human being must be the only animal who would deliberately expose its own offspring to risks of this kind. But if something frightened the dog and he dragged the pram and child in front of oncoming traffic, it would be the dog to blame! It is no good saying your dog would not do that. No one knows what a dog, or a person for that matter, will do in unforeseen circumstances. In any case, if a dog can be relied on not to pull a pram over, he can also be relied on to lie down and stay with the pram without needing to be tied to it.

Jumping up

Nothing is more infuriating than a dog which greets you, or your friends, by leaping all over you. This is especially annoying if you are wearing your best clothes and the dog has muddy paws. Dogs do not differentiate between good and old clothes; or whether or not their paws are muddy. So, you must teach your dog not to jump up, irrespective of what you are wearing.

It is best to start right at the beginning by never fussing a puppy when he jumps up to greet you. Push him down gently but firmly and praise him very well *when he is on the ground*. And try to train your friends to do the same—which may prove much more difficult! A common mistake people make, especially children, is to raise their hands. To the tune of 'get down, get down' they wave their hands around like the conductor of an orchestra, which only encourages the puppy to jump even more, with excitement. Keep your hands down and scold the puppy with a firm 'no'. Don't use the command 'down' if that is the command you use to make the puppy lie down; it will only confuse him.

If a dog has acquired the habit of leaping up, the best correction is to raise your knee and catch him in the chest as he jumps. One has to be fairly active to do this properly but it does not require any great skill. And there is little risk of creating the wrong association of ideas. If you bring your knee up as the dog leaps he won't see what hit him and will think that he has hurt himself. The harder he leaps, the more he will hurt himself, and some dogs can be cured in one lesson. With others the lesson must be repeated until he eventually gets the message. You are not trying to stop him from greeting you, just from jumping up, so don't forget to make a great fuss of him when he is back on all fours.

For the less boisterous dog that stands up rather than jumps up, treading on his hind feet, one after the other, with your toe will make him move backwards. Again praise him well

Far left: As the dog leaps up bring the knee up smartly to catch him in the chest so that he feels he has hurt himself.

Left: For the dog that stands up on you, tread gently on his hind feet one after the other until he goes down.

when he is on the ground, but don't excite him too much or he will leap up again.

Fighting

Fighting is a problem which often arises through the guarding instinct. The dog wants to protect his own property, be it his owner or his territory, and will attack any dog that he considers a threat. Often he is encouraged to attack other dogs by the actions of his owner. Every day, one sees dog owners with the dog in one hand and a stick or umbrella in the other. If a strange dog approaches, probably a very friendly dog, they swipe or poke at it in an effort to 'shoo it off'. However, the pack instinct makes the dog want to join in his leader's activities. Any self-respecting dog will be only too delighted to assist his owner in seeing off a strange dog. These owners effectively teach their dogs to attack other dogs—and then wonder why their dogs are so aggressive! Added to this is the fact that many dogs are much more aggressive on a leash than when free.

In the natural state it is very rare for an adult dog to attack a submissive member of the pack. If he attacked a puppy the mother, aided by other members of the pack, would attack and possibly kill him. But some domestic dogs are so far removed from nature that they will attack a puppy, females more often than males. It is seldom, however, that they hurt a puppy

seriously and it is usually fairly safe to allow a puppy to
approach any dog which appears friendly towards it. Indeed, he
should be encouraged to do so, which is one advantage of those
training classes which allow young puppies to be taken along as
'spectators'. A puppy which mixes regularly with other dogs as
he grows up is much less likely to be aggressive than one that is
kept on his own.

Some dogs, like some people, are just born pugilists, to whom
the protection of property or territory does not enter into it.
They simply enjoy fighting. And it must be remembered that
there are dog owners who derive sadistic pleasure from seeing
their own dogs sorting out all the other dogs in the neighbour-
hood, which would be bad enough if it ended there. But many a
well-behaved, law-abiding dog that has been attacked and
forced into a fight by one of these 'hooligans' has been turned
into an inveterate fighter in the course of that one fight.

Which brings us to yet another type of fighting dog—the
nervous fighter. This type fights because he is afraid that he
may be attacked. Like the nervous person, he completely loses
his head and wades in.

If there is a certain cure for a real fighter, we have not yet
found it. Some dogs do give up fighting if they are nearly killed
by a more powerful adversary. But very often they are completely broken in spirit and undergo a change in character.
And in organized dog fights (illegal, but unfortunately still
taking place in some countries) many animals are killed, or
nearly killed. Once the latter have been patched up and time
allowed for their wounds to heal they will enter into the fray
with even greater ferocity.

If you have purchased a puppy with a good, sound temperament, and brought him up on the lines suggested in this book,
fighting should not be one of your problems. Any tendency to
fight whilst still a youngster should have been sharply corrected. In exactly the same way as any other signs of aggression
were nipped in the bud. As already mentioned, most dogs that
fight are more aggressive on the leash than off. When on the leash
they are invariably insistent pullers—straining to attack other
dogs. But if the dog has been thoroughly trained to walk quietly
on a slack leash, he cannot at the same time be rushing forward
towards every dog he sees. So the short answer is to teach your
dog to be obedient.

However, if you should be unlucky enough to be out walking
with your dog and he becomes involved in a fight, *don't panic*. It
will only make things worse. Few dogs dash in and take a really
good grip on another dog immediately. To start with, there is
usually a great deal of growling, snarling and snapping. Which
should give you and the owner of the other dog (assuming his

owner is with him) time to do something about it. Quickly, but quietly take hold of your dog by the collar, the other owner doing the same with his dog, and quietly but firmly drag them apart. If the two dogs do get hold of each other, use as much force as necessary to choke the dog into letting go his hold. If the dog is wearing an ordinary leather-buckled collar try to twist the collar to get the same effect. Once you have the dogs apart make sure you keep them apart, using a very severe tone of voice as well as the collar and leash to bring the dog back under control. Never, never pull two dogs apart. The most terrible injuries can be inflicted if a large dog has a hold on a small one and is dragged off him. And do not try hitting the dogs, you will probably miss, get bitten yourself and give the dogs more encouragement.

As already mentioned, every effort should be made to introduce your puppy to as many other dogs as possible whilst he is still at the submissive age. And always try to avoid circumstances likely to lead to fights. Most important of all, don't encourage your dog to fight—consciously or unconsciously.

It is worth mentioning that dogs of the first two categories are often great characters. Almost invariably they are good with children, puppies and other young animals. Not so the nervous fighter, which is very often the dog which bites a child or attacks a puppy for the same reason that he fights. He is afraid that the child *might* be going to poke him in the eye or the puppy bite his ear!

Castration is sometimes recommended as a means of reducing the tendency to fight, and in some cases it has almost miraculous results. But not invariably. Castration tends to reduce a dog's dominance, his instinct to lead the pack, which of course is closely allied to his desire to protect the pack by challenging any intruders. This makes many dogs fight, and when that is the case castration is likely to prove very effective. But it will do nothing to improve the nervous fighter, which will still be just as nervous. In an earlier chapter we recommended the castration of all dogs not intended for breeding. So far as fighting is concerned, the operation will never make the dog worse and may well make him better.

So far we have discussed the inclination to fight between male dogs and some people have the idea that females don't fight. True, they are less inclined to start fights, but when they do fight they often prove that the female really is more deadly than the male! Most breeders know that two males will often have a good scrap, then make it up. But if two females develop a hate for each other, they will seize every opportunity to get at each other's throats for the rest of their lives.

Other pets and babies

A problem that worries a great many dog owners is how their dog will react to other pet or domestic animals. This depends to a great extent on the dog himself and the other animal; so we shall try to deal with several cases.

Let's start with the new puppy in a home where the pet cat is already established. Cats vary enormously in their behaviour and are notoriously unpredictable. Your cat may attack the puppy viciously, sit and stare at him or climb up the curtains to get out of his reach! The puppy will be more predictable and will, almost certainly, want to investigate this strange, new animal.

The first essential is to keep both puppy and cat under control until you find how they are going to react to each other. Don't on any account allow the puppy to chase the cat or tease it by bouncing and yapping at it. Many cats have taught puppies to leave them well alone. But a hefty swipe from a dominant cat could be accepted as a challenge (especially by an older dog) and will have the opposite from the desired effect. It is well known that many terriers won't kill rats until they have been bitten by one, when they immediately become obsessed with killing them. Provided the cat is amiable and the puppy is kept under control, there is rarely any problem. However, the older the puppy, the more care will have to be taken.

Some dogs will resent a cat brought into their home; but here again much depends on the attitude of the cat. Most dogs are completely taken aback by the bold, fearless cat or kitten that

Make every effort to keep everything under control when introducing strange animals.

walks straight up to them, purring. The bold, tough dog, which probably chases cats off his own territory, is unlikely to resent this approach. It is the nervous, timid dog that is likely to attack.

It is a common fallacy that dogs and cats are natural enemies. It is cats and dog owners who are often natural enemies. Many dog owners take a sadistic delight in seeing their dogs chase other people's cats, knowing full well that the cats' owners cherish them just as much as they do their dog.

The pet rabbit, guinea pig or similar pet is less likely to cause trouble than the cat, despite the fact that the dog *is* its natural enemy. Unlike sheep, which have retained their natural fear of dogs, most domestic rabbits show no fear at all, so they should not panic or try to run away—we have in mind the really tame pet rabbit that is allowed to run around the house or garden. Because the rabbit does not run away, you will be able to correct your dog as severely as necessary should he try to molest it. Make sure you keep the dog on the leash, be ready for any reaction but don't give the dog the impression that you are expecting any trouble.

The most serious of all problems which many dog owners have to face comes with the arrival of a new baby. The parents are unlikely to regard this as another animal, but the dog almost certainly will—and, of course, he will be right! This is one instance where you will come upon one of the few canine characteristics which really is almost human—jealousy. When you consider how many human beings, with the ability to reason, commit suicides, murders and other terrible acts because of jealousy, you should be able to sympathize with the dog. Unfortunately, many people do not. If he shows the slightest sign of resentment, they accuse him of having 'turned nasty', and very often become nasty to him. Which, of course, only makes the situation worse.

But we must also sympathize with the parents, especially the mother, who will be instinctively protective towards her offspring. It is not the love and affection she lavishes on the baby that causes the problem. It is her changed attitude towards the dog. Having brought him up as a friend she now almost shuns him and he resents it, just as an older child frequently does.

So the first, and most important thing, is the right attitude towards the dog. Try to ensure that he does not feel left out, but instead, that the baby is his as well as yours. Quite often young couples acquire a puppy when they set up house and then produce a baby when the dog is two or three years old. In the meantime, no effort is made to introduce the dog to small children. The vast majority of dogs like children if they are introduced to them as puppies—provided they are not nervous

When picking up a puppy, always put one hand underneath to support the weight.

and the children are not unkind. So try to take your puppy to play with your friends' children—which will, at least, give you some idea of how he is likely to react when yours arrives. Many dogs, including tough, dominant ones, adore babies and will sometimes become very protective towards them. Unfortunately, there are others which just cannot control their jealousy. To force such a dog to share a home with a child that he loathes and detests is very cruel to the dog and puts a great mental strain on the parents. And it is also very dangerous, as is proved by the tragedies which occasionally occur. The only sensible thing to do in such circumstances is to find another home for the dog. And, of course, no dog should ever be left alone with a small baby.

4 Obedience training

So far, the main object has been to bring up the puppy so that he causes the least possible trouble—to prevent bad habits rather than to do any actual training. But, as we have already emphasized, dogs want to be trained. Trained dogs are invariably happier than untrained ones—and they usually have happier owners too.

Great satisfaction can be derived from training a dog, and it is not nearly as time-consuming as people imagine. Most of the training can be done while you are exercising the dog and if you have not time to do that, you should not keep a dog.

Training classes are now established in most countries and undoubtedly contribute to the better training of dogs. Nevertheless, it must be remembered that a training class is only as good as its instructor. Many people are regarded as experts when they have trained one dog of one breed to a very high standard. Faced with a difficult dog they would not know where

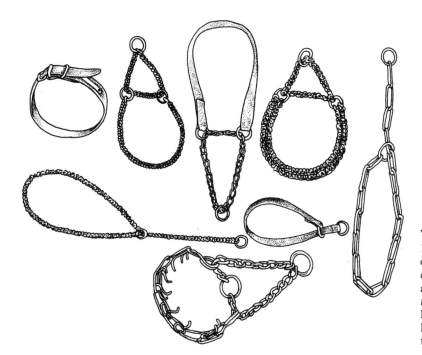

Various types of collars.
Top row, left to right: buckled leather or nylon; double-action, single chain; double-action nylon; double-action, double chain. *Middle row, left to right*: chain slip with watch-chain links; nylon slip; chain slip with large links. *Bottom*: continental training collar.

to start. We know this from experience, as nearly all the people who come to us for personal advice have already been to training classes. And some of the advice they have been given is quite appalling.

One great advantage of classes is that they accustom a puppy or young dog to meeting other dogs. They also give owners an opportunity to meet people with a common interest, and sometimes a common problem! And if you have a competitive nature, you may want to train for competitions.

Training methods vary just as much as dogs and their owners do. There are, however, several generally accepted exercises which form a useful basis for most dogs and most owners. If you have brought your puppy up on the lines recommended, you will find these exercises much easier and, of course, if you have allowed him to develop bad habits you will find them that much more difficult. Before starting any exercises, the dog must be friendly towards you and be accustomed to a collar and leash.

Heelwork

At one time, the first exercise we taught was always heelwork. Experience has forced us to change our minds on this. For the keen, headstrong young dog, especially if he has had no previous training, we still regard heelwork as the best foundation on which to start. However, the naturally obedient dog that already follows to heel of his own accord can be (and we believe, often is) completely soured of all training by being jerked about on the end of a leash. That heelwork is not essential to obedience is proved by the hundreds of good working sheep-dogs, which have never had a collar on their necks. It is, however, essential in obedience competitions. The kind of dog who is likely to do well in competitions will need either some heelwork lessons or, at least, to take to them willingly. So we shall start with this exercise.

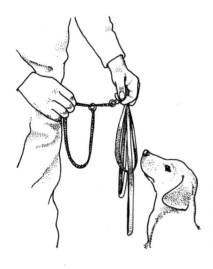

Preparing to put on a single-action slip collar.

Everyone knows the advantage of a dog which walks properly to heel—or at least the disadvantages of one that does not. What is not so often realized, is that the main object of this exercise, is to get the dog's mind to co-ordinate with the trainer's actions and tone of voice. Once that is achieved, the other exercises become much easier, and in the process he should learn to walk properly to heel.

As with all exercises, start in a familiar place where it is unlikely that there will be any distractions. If you are using a chain slip collar, use one of the watch-chain type. And be sure you put it on correctly. To do so, face the dog and, with the ring to which the leash is attached held in the left hand, slip the

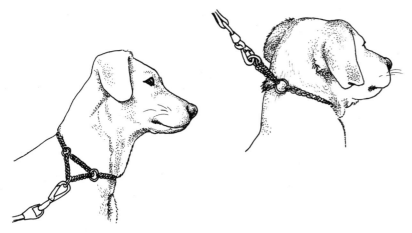

Far left: Double-action slip collar hanging loose when the lead is slack.

Left: A double-action slip collar fitting neatly round the dog's neck when the leash is tightened.

chain noose over the dog's head. This means that the ring through which the chain slips comes under the dog's neck. When the dog is on your left side, you can then jerk the chain up quickly. Just as important, it will instantly fall slack when you slacken the leash. If you put it on the wrong way, the ring will come over the dog's neck and tend to stay there when you slacken the leash.

The next essential is a strong, pliable leash about $1\frac{1}{2}$–2 m (5–$6\frac{1}{2}$ ft) long. Having got the collar comfortably on the dog, stand facing the same directions as he is, with him on your left side. Hold the leash in your right hand with your elbow bent at a right angle. Allow the leash to be long enough for the loop, where it bends, to hang about half way between the dog's neck and the ground. And always keep in mind that the right hand is the correcting one and the left hand the rewarding one.

Now, move off quickly, saying the dog's name followed by a sharp 'heel'. It is unlikely that the dog will move as quickly, and you can automatically jerk him with the right hand. This should bring him up to you, when you must immediately reward him, caressing and fussing him with the left hand. This is easy with a big dog, whose head is just about level with your hand but not so easy with a little dog.

If the dog is a 'puller' who rushes forward on the lead, let him go, and at the exact moment when he is about to reach the end, turn sharp right, give a sharp 'heel' and at the same time jerk with the right hand so that you have your own strength combined with his in the jerk. Keep on turning, at right angles and right about turns, jerking him around but never forgetting to praise and encourage with your left hand. Pat your thigh, stroke his cheek, or do anything else that you find will bring him closer to you. In obstinate cases, you can occasionally turn left and 'crash' into the dog, but too much of this will tend to keep him away from you rather than bring him closer.

Heel work with the dog in the correct position, with his head level with his handler's knee. Note the left (rewarding) hand encouraging the dog to keep close and the right (correcting) hand ready to give him a sharp jerk if he wanders off. Note also the slack loop on the leash.

Keep all your movements brisk and alive. Keep turning in different directions so that the dog never knows which way you will turn next. Don't work to a set plan, and remember that, as well as getting the dog to keep close to you, you are trying to make him concentrate on your actions. This he should do when he finds that every time his mind wanders he receives a sharp jerk, but that when he pays attention he will be praised and fussed.

If you are unfortunate enough to have a dog which lags, you will have to do much more rewarding than correcting and give very short spells of training.

Obviously the degree of jerking varies enormously from dog to dog. If one were to give a terrific jerk on a chain slip collar to a sensitive thin-skinned dog, like a Whippet, it would amount to downright cruelty and the dog would probably crumple up and go to pieces. On the other hand, if one gave a little jerk to which a Whippet would respond to a big powerful young German Shepherd Dog, which had been pulling his owner all over the place since he was three months old, he simply would not feel it. With a big strong dog a good deal of physical strength is necessary in the initial stages, which is one reason why many owners, especially ladies, put in a tremendous amount of work with no results.

In this exercise we have found that rewarding with food does no permanent good, and may do harm. It will make a dog keep up with you as long as you have food in your hand, but that is not allowed in competitions. And one cannot go around constantly offering up bits of meat. A very few trainers do sometimes use food as a reward in heelwork, but it should only be used as a last resort.

You may now have your dog doing heelwork very well on the lead. He keeps right up alongside your left leg to receive encouragement from your left hand, and turns sharply to the right when you turn, in order to avoid a sharp jerk on the leash. If he does these things—but not unless he does—you can try some 'heel free'. Here you are likely to find out whether or not you have been training correctly. If you have, and you have the right dog, he will do his heelwork just the same off the lead as on it. If, on the other hand, you have been jerking at him in a lifeless, mechanical way, without rewarding him at the right time, he will probably follow you somehow, either well behind or away to your left. In this case, put the leash back on and start again, encouraging him to respond to the left hand and only using the right one if that fails. Don't forget that when you take the leash off, you still have your left hand for encouragement, but your right—correcting—hand is gone.

Some dogs, when the leash is removed, make a dash for freedom even if they have been doing heelwork on the leash quite well. Fortunately, they almost invariably rush ahead, which gives you the opportunity to apply correction at exactly the right time—if you are quick enough! Halt, as usual, with the dog on the leash, remove it and hold both ends in your right hand, so that the leash hangs in a loop by your side, where the dog cannot see it. Now start off smartly in the same way and with the same commands as before. Try to keep the dog to your left side with encouragement but, if he is the type of dog we have in mind, he will walk a few steps and then, without any warning, shoot off like an arrow. As he does so, not before nor after, give him a 'stinger' on the hind quarters with the leash. He should, and almost invariably will, stop dead and rush back to you for 'protection', when you must praise him very well. No dog, even the boldest, likes being hit by something out of the blue.

Although this method sounds easy, it has snags. Firstly, you have only a split second in which to act, so it will test your powers of concentration and your ability to anticipate what the dog is going to do. Secondly, it will test your ability to praise your dog instantly when he does the right thing. If you miss him but he has not noticed that you tried to hit him you will have done neither good nor harm, and can try again. But if he sees you take a swipe at him and you miss, you will be further back than before you started. So it is all up to you. And do not forget to give a sharp 'heel' as you go to hit him, so that when next you say 'heel' as he decides to go, he will associate it with that sudden smack which 'descended from Heaven'. Instead of running away he should come closer to you.

Don't keep on saying 'heel, heel, heel'. Don't ever give a command unless you are in a position to see that it is obeyed. This is, again, association of ideas. The object is to make the dog associate 'heel' with correction (a jerk), in anticipation of which he will respond to the sound. You enforce this by getting him to associate coming close to you with reward, in anticipation of which, he should want to come of his own accord. Whether or not he responds more to the correction or the reward depends chiefly on the dog himself. Most dogs respond in varying degrees to both, but remember that, providing he has done something to deserve it, you cannot over-reward a dog. However, a sensitive dog can be completely upset by over-correction.

Sit at the halt

As soon as the dog is walking on a loose leash and coming up close to you in response to encouragement from your left hand, you can start teaching him to sit automatically every time you halt. There are several ways to make a dog sit (it is not usually very difficult) and we use either of two methods.

For the first one, have the dog moving smartly, in the correct position close to you. Stop suddenly, at the same time giving the command 'sit', swing your body round to the left (don't move your feet) and move your right hand over his head. About 50 per cent of dogs will look up at the trainer's right hand and, when the movements are combined with a sudden halt, will sit down on their haunches. The whole thing must be carried out simultaneously from a walk. It is no use stopping and then moving your right hand in the hope that the dog will sit. It must be done *as* you halt.

You might, however, have the other sort of dog, which will just stand and look at you as though you had gone mad! In this case, you will have to force him into a sitting position by pulling back on his collar with your right hand, at the same time pressing on his rump with your left. Make sure he sits square on his haunches or on his right side, which brings him in towards you. If he is obstinate, you can grip the loose skin on his rump with your left hand. The first method is much easier than the second. And, being firm believers in doing everything the easiest way, we always try it first, and only use the second if that fails.

Whichever method you use, don't forget to praise the dog very well whenever he sits, and try to get him close up to you right from the start. If he sits wide do not move towards him.

Far left: Teaching the dog to sit automatically at the halt. The trainer swings his body towards the dog and lifts his hand right over the dog's head.

Left: Teaching the dog to sit from the standing position by pushing down on the rump with the left hand and at the same time pulling back on the leash with the right.

Move to the right, away from him and coax him up with your left hand. If necessary, swing his haunches to you with the same hand, as he sits down. Never move towards your dog, except when returning to him from a sit or down. Always make him move towards you. Don't keep on pushing him gently into a sitting position every time you halt. It will teach him nothing and will only get him used to being pushed down. Be gentle to start with, but if you get no response, gradually replace the push with a slap on the rump.

A dog must not only do what you want, he must do it quickly. A dog that is slow and stubborn on his sits can often be improved by combining both methods. Stop suddenly, swing the right hand over the dog and, with the end of the leash that is held in the other hand, give him a sharp smack on the rump. Never forget to praise him when he sits—especially the first time he shows any inclination to sit on his own.

In all heelwork make your movements quick and alive. It is a good idea to repeat each exercise several times until the dog grasps what is wanted. For instance:

1. You halt, say 'sit', push the dog into a sitting position and praise him.

2. You halt, say 'sit' and as you go to push him he sits himself; praise very well.

3. You halt, say 'sit' very firmly and he does so of his own accord. Praise very well indeed and either go on to another exercise or finish for the day.

It is unlikely that he will do it as soon as the third time but that is the idea, which can also be applied to the right turns and about turns. Repeat each exercise until you see some sign of response, praise very well and leave it for the day. Next day you will be able to start where you left off, and so will steadily progress. If you just keep on and on, the dog will become bored and you will be further back than when you started.

Sit and stay

Before starting this exercise, do a little heelwork to settle the dog down. Now halt with your dog sitting at heel. Keeping the leash in the right hand, move very slowly round to face him, saying very firmly, but not in a scolding tone, 'sit—stay'. Now move back a couple of steps and pause. If he remains sitting go back to him immediately, before he has time to get up, and praise him very well for having stayed there. Repeat this a few times, then move a little to the right and a little to the left, so that gradually he will allow you to move right round him, which he will probably not like to begin with.

We usually finish the first lesson at this stage, and it is important not to make any hasty or jerky movements. If he starts to get up, take hold of him quickly by the collar (before he has time to get on his feet) and with your hand under his chin, pull his head up towards you, and then force him back on his haunches, at the same time saying 'sit' in an angry tone. And don't forget to praise him when he does sit.

For the next stage start as before, but when you go back to him slip the leash quietly on to the ground and move back again, this time without the leash. Keep moving away from him, a little further each time, always returning to praise him for sitting. Concentrate on the dog and try to hold his concentration by raising your hand and moving it to attract his attention should he look away. When you are able to walk away some distance try turning your back, but glance over your shoulder, as many dogs will get up the first time you turn your back on them. If your dog does get up, go back as fast as you can and sit him quickly on exactly the spot where you left him.

Should he go down on the sit, go back to him, and, holding your hand above your head, tap him gently on his toes with your toe, at the same time telling him to sit. You may have to put the leash back on and hold it in the hand above his head. Don't just heave him up into a sitting position nor stamp on his toes with your big foot. Encourage him to sit up on his own with the aid of the leash and tapping on his toes. Be careful not to rush back to your dog in a way that will frighten him. Go back as quickly as possible but do it quietly, or he will get up and run away when he sees you coming.

The most severe correction it is possible to give a dog is to lift him right off his feet and shake him. Here a dog is being 'ticked off' for disobedience much more effectively than any amount of smacking or beating.

You will have noticed (or we hope you will) that you have not at this stage called the dog to you at all. The most important rule of all for success in this exercise is never to recall the dog until he is quite steady on his sits and downs.

Never try to teach a dog to stay while you are out of sight until he is quite steady while you are in sight. Here again, the secret of success is to progress gradually. Begin by moving quietly but quickly round a corner, behind a tree or whatever happens to be handy, and coming back almost immediately. Many dogs get up the instant the handler goes out of sight for the first time, but they get such a surprise if he returns and scolds them that they are far less likely to do it again the next time. From then on, gradually increase the length of time, never forgetting to praise the dog when you return.

Down

Whether you are training your dog for your own pleasure or for competition work, one of the most important of all exercises is the down. It is worth noting that this is the one and only exercise which is taught to the average sheepdog before he is allowed to work sheep.

No great skill is required in teaching a dog to lie down. It is just a matter of forcing him to the ground and making sure he stays there. The easiest way to do this with a big strong dog is illustrated below. With the leash running under the instep of the left foot pull up with right hand at the same time pushing the dog down with the left one. Once he is down, keep your foot close enough to his collar to prevent him from getting up.

Making a dog lie down with the leash being pulled under the instep with the right hand. Left hand is simultaneously pushing down on the dog's withers. Make sure that the lead is long enough to allow for give and take.

The important point is to get him to associate lying down with the command 'down' or with a hand signal. As you push him down give the command in a harsh tone. Most dogs, if spoken to harshly, will naturally creep or lie right down. Full use should always be made of any natural tendency such as this. Don't worry about him being cowed. He will soon get over it once he understands what you want him to do.

The other important point is to praise him when he stays down. Some trainers disagree on this, maintaining that to praise a dog in this exercise will make him get up. This can be true in the early stages, but it can be overcome by balancing correction with reward. You should then have a happy dog, which stays down to please you, not a miserable one, which stays down because he is afraid to get up. So long as he struggles, keep telling him 'down' and force him to do so—gently if he is a sensitive dog. But if he decides to be rough with you, you will have to be rough back. But immediately he relaxes, for even a second, change your tone of voice and tactics completely and praise him very well but quietly. If you get him too excited he will probably just get up again. Don't give him the chance to start struggling again. Let him up and start again at the beginning. Very soon (the time varies from dog to dog) he should go down on command, assisted by a slight push, and should stay down beside you.

From there continue exactly as with the 'sit–stay', until you can walk round him, step over him, run away from him, run past him, jump over him and make all sorts of odd noises! What you are trying to do is make the dog understand that no matter what happens, he must stay there until you tell him to get up. If he does get up, go back to him quickly but quietly, not frightening him, but at the same time letting him know that you are very, very angry, and put him down firmly in exactly the same spot. This is very important and it is worth making a mental note of a stone, twig or tuft of grass beside the place where he is lying. Do not put something down beside him, or he may learn to stay beside an object belonging to you, and might not stay without it. Teach the dog to stay down out of sight in the same way that you have taught him to stay sitting.

If you have any ambitions to take part in competitions, don't teach him to go down from the sit, or give a lesson on the down immediately after one on the sit. Either tends to make a dog go down on the sit, a very difficult fault to eradicate. Any similar exercises, likely to be confusing to the dog, should be taught quite separately. For example, give a lesson on the down, then some heelwork, then the sit. Or give a lesson on the down in the morning and one on the sit in the afternoon.

Far too many people train their dogs with one object in

view—winning competitions. They swot up all the exercises in the particular test and go through them in the same order, day after day, until the dog does them automatically—in the same way as a performing dog goes through his routine. A clever dog soon learns which exercise follows which, and will, if allowed, carry on without any commands at all. If people would forget about competitions and teach their dogs obedience they would get on much better. In particular, if they would teach them to go down and stay down, in any place and under all sorts of conditions, they would find that they would stay in the obedience ring—or anywhere else.

If you have just started a lesson by ordering your dog to 'down' and the telephone rings, never go away and leave him and forget about him. He should stay there until you return, but he probably won't so don't take the risk. Slip the leash back on and take him with you, making him lie down beside you, where you can keep an eye on him. In any case it is very good for the dog to become accustomed to lying beside you for quite long periods before you ask him to stay when you move away. This need not take the form of a set exercise. When you are having a meal, watching television, or reading the newspaper put a leash on the dog and make him lie down close to your feet. He will have no option but to stay there. Half an hour to an hour of this every day will do far more to steady a restless, fidgety dog than taking him to classes once a week.

Once the dog will lie down on command when close to you, he should be taught to drop on command, even when some distance away from you. Many dogs have been killed when returning to their owners across a road. If they had been taught to drop at the side of the road their lives could have been saved.

It is a good idea to make a dog lie still for quite long periods.

They must learn to drop instantly. It is no good if they move two or three metres after you have shouted 'down' and lie down in the middle of the road!

Start by calling the dog to you and give him the command 'down' just as he reaches you. Gradually drop him further and further away. If he does not stop, don't just stand there saying 'down, down, down' while he creeps forward to lie down at your feet. If he does not drop on the first command rush towards him, take him firmly by the collar and put him down on the exact spot where he should have dropped. This exercise is best carried out when out for a walk with the dog running free. Once he will drop coming to you, practise dropping him when he is going away. Make the whole thing a game until the dog will drop instantly at any time and in any place. And remember that any dog that will always come when called and lie down when told to (and stay there) is under control.

Recall to handler

We have already dealt at some length with how to get a young puppy to come when called. The same principles apply to an older dog when you are teaching him the 'recall'. They may not work with a dog that has developed the habit of running off when called, but they should do if you have brought your pup up on the lines suggested. Presuming that your dog is steady on the sits and downs when you are in sight, sit him in the usual way, walk away from him and then turn to face him. Call his name pleasantly and he should come to you. Most people call the dog's name followed by a command—'come' or 'here'. It should be used in a praising tone of voice, combined, in the early stages, with moving your hands in front of you and patting your thighs in encouragement.

For competition work you don't just want your dog to come to you. You want him to come at the gallop and sit smartly in front of you. To achieve this concentrate on getting the dog to come to you (even if he knocks you over in the process) before worrying too much about the sit and finish. The easiest way we know to persuade a dog to come, at the double, is to offer him food. This is the only exercise in which we always use food as a reward in training. Every now and again we use it to speed up a trained dog and we always use it when working in film or TV studios. Never give food to the dog until he is in the exact position in which you want him. Hold the food in your hand, tempt him when he comes to you and move backwards—again, never move towards your dog—until you have him in the right position. Now order him to sit and when he does so give him the food. Do that two or three times with a greedy dog and he should bound straight up to you, tail wagging, and sit down, right in front of you, eyes and ears alert. With a less greedy dog it may not work so well, but food nearly always helps and cannot do any harm if used as directed.

Be careful not to allow your dog to come before he is called as some dogs quickly develop the habit of getting up as soon as you turn to face them. If your dog does come before you call him put him back immediately, walk away again and turn to face him as before. Stand facing him for a minute or two, then go back to him and praise him very well for having stayed in position. Do this several times before you call him again, try to make him understand that when you walk away and turn to face him it does not always mean that you are going to call him.

With a difficult dog a light check cord can be useful. When teaching an easy dog there is one object in view—making him do what you want. But in teaching a difficult dog there are two—making him do what you want and (often far more difficult) preventing him from doing what he wants! For the latter purpose the check cord can be very useful. But don't use it as a means of dragging the dog to you, only as a means of preventing him from running away. Reward him by tone of voice, food, and so on in the same way as if you were not using a line.

In competition, after most exercises, a dog has to 'finish', which means he moves from a sitting position in front of the handler to a sitting position at heel, by the handler's left side. If you wish to teach this, the most usual way is for the dog to move to the handler's right, go round his back and finish up facing forward sitting on his left. Some dogs appear to need no teaching for this exercise at all, whilst others are very slow to grasp what is wanted. Once the penny has dropped, however, it is rarely that the exercise causes any trouble. However, plenty of practice is needed for speed and smartness.

Sit the dog facing you with the leash attached. Move backwards about two paces, giving the command 'heel', followed by a jerk on the leash with the right hand. This will bring the dog to his feet, and there should be a distinct movement of the hand as you will use it as a signal after you have discarded the leash. Having got the dog on his feet, move forward again, at the same time bringing the dog round your back and changing the leash from your right to your left hand. When the dog comes up to your left hand, halt and he should sit, as he has been doing in ordinary heelwork. Continue on these lines with the leash on, gradually reducing the backwards and forwards movements until all that is necessary is a slight movement from the right hand. Next, discard the leash and continue until you can stand quite still and the dog will go smartly to heel with one command only. Some people teach this exercise with food, but unless you are careful it can do more harm than good, as the dog is inclined to go right round the handler and finish up where he started, sitting in front looking for a tit bit.

The stand

For competitions it is necessary to teach the dog to stand, and the same applies if you want to show him in 'beauty' or 'conformation' classes. There are several methods of teaching this exercise and we shall attempt to describe two of them.

Start with the dog walking to heel on the leash. Halt slowly and say 'sta-and'. At the same time, put the right hand in front of the dog's face, palm open and simultaneously draw the left hand along the flank. If he tries to sit, use the left hand to prevent him doing so. All the movements should be smooth and the command should be given slowly. Any jerkiness or an abrupt command will tend to make the dog sit, which has already been taught anyhow.

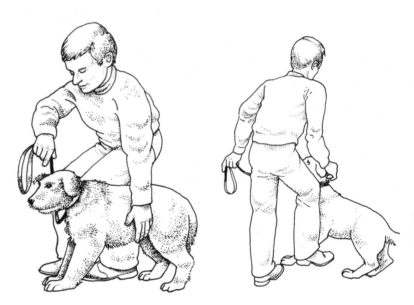

Right: Here the left hand is placed in the dog's flank to keep him on his feet.

Far right: The leash in the left hand is encouraging the dog to move and the toe of the right foot is under him to discourage him from sitting down.

In the second method, start with the dog lying down, with you facing his right side, leash in the right hand. Now give the command to stand and with the aid of the leash coax him to his feet. As he rises, push the toe of your left foot gently under his right flank, from where it can be pushed right under his belly if he tries to sit or lie down. If the dog tends to move away as your foot approaches start with him up against a wall.

As with the sits and downs, once the dog understands the command to stand it is only a question of practice until he will stand and allow you to walk away from him. We use food as a reward in this exercise and try to teach all our dogs to stand back from us and catch food thrown to them. Some dogs do this naturally and some find it very difficult, but it makes all the difference in the show ring. That is for those who show their dogs on slack leads standing on their own four feet, but not for those who grovel around on their knees treating their poor animals as objects, not dogs!

5 Applied training

Retrieving

Here we have an exercise which may require no training at all, or which you might find the most difficult one to teach—depending more on your dog than your training ability.

Most training authorities will tell you that there are two methods of teaching the retrieve—the dog can be taught in play or by the forcing method. It is more accurate to say that a dog can be taught to retrieve by the forcing method or encouraged to use his natural retrieving instinct. Whether or not the dog will ever be reliable if he is taught in play depends entirely on the strength of this instinct. In some dogs, particularly gundog breeds, the retrieving instinct is so strong that it often makes it difficult to stop a dog picking up anything you throw. Such dogs can become quite reliable without having to resort to the more difficult forcing method.

We always try to teach a dog in play, but if we find the dog is not going to be reliable, we change to the forcing method. Often we end up using both, the extent to which each is used depending on the dog. So first try to teach the dog in play. In other words, develop the instinct which we hope is already there.

The retrieving instinct is closely associated with the hunting instinct. A gundog retrieving a pheasant for his handler is not so very different from a fox taking a chicken home to its den. A dog derives his greatest pleasure from following his instincts. By doing so, he finds his own reward and, if allowed (it cannot be forced), becomes keener and keener. On the other hand, if an instinct is not allowed to develop it will remain dormant or may even die out. It is often easy to kill it outright by suppression in the early stages of development. This can be very useful, for instance in stopping a puppy from chasing bikes. But many people unthinkingly kill an instinct (in the seedling stage) which they later want to develop. If, therefore, your puppy brings you your best hat in triumph, don't scold him. Take it from him gently (it will do the hat less harm anyway) praise him very well, and put it out of his reach.

The age at which you start teaching the retrieve in play depends on the age at which the retrieving instinct shows signs of developing. If the puppy shows an inclination to pick up and carry objects, no harm will be done by starting when he is quite a baby, providing that you do only play with him and never keep on until he is bored. Never try to force him (you won't be able to anyhow), just encourage him if, and when he feels like it.

To do this, get him really excited and throw the object away from you. Use something the puppy likes and throw it along the ground, not up in the air. The hunting instinct should make him chase the moving object and the retrieving instinct, if present, will make him pick it up. But it may not make him bring it back to you. Don't, on any account, run after him. Run away from him and it is more than likely that he will come after you with the object in his mouth. If he tries to keep hold of it don't try to pull it out of his mouth. Many pups will release an object if offered food as an alternative. This makes the puppy open his mouth and also acts as a reward for retrieving. If it does not work, catch hold of the puppy, place the left hand across his muzzle and very, very gently press his lips against his teeth. At the same time tell him firmly to 'drop it' and praise him very well the instant he lets go. Many dogs taught to retrieve in play spit the object out at the feet of their handlers. To overcome this, you will have to combine this method with the forcing one, teaching the dog to hold the object as will be explained shortly.

Thousands of pet dogs, with no training at all, retrieve all sorts of objects to owners who have no idea how to train them—and they show much more enthusiasm than many dogs seen in the obedience rings. There are two reasons for this. Firstly, like everything else the average pet dog wants to do, he does it without suppression or control of any sort. Secondly, the dog realizes that if he brings the object back to his owner he will be rewarded by having it thrown again. This provides him with the pleasure of following his hunting and retrieving instincts. They, in turn, will become stronger with use, sometimes becoming an obsession if no control is effected.

Suppose that your new puppy will not retrieve in play, either because the retrieving instinct is too weak or because it was not encouraged when it first showed signs of developing. It should still be possible to teach the retrieve by the forcing method. In fact some trainers start off with this method whether the puppy will or will not retrieve in play. Don't start the forcing method with a young puppy. Nine months is quite young enough even with a forward youngster, and it has the advantage that it can be used with a dog that is past the playful stage. The object used universally in training circles is a wooden dumb-bell of a size

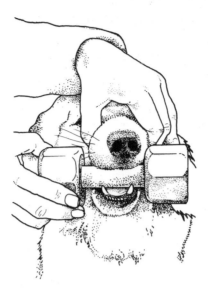

Retrieving Stage 1: Persuading the dog to accept a dumb-bell by gently pressing the lips against his teeth until he opens his mouth.

and weight appropriate to the dog. This is used because it is so easy for the dog to pick up and for the trainer to put into the dog's mouth.

Don't start teaching the retrieve until you have instilled some sort of obedience into your dog. It is no good trying to make a dog hold a dumb-bell if, at the same time, he is struggling to break away from you. Complete obedience is not necessary but he must be able to sit still and pay attention. Otherwise you are trying to teach two things at once.

With your dog on the leash, sit him in the usual position at your left side. Put your left hand over the dog's face and gently press the lips against the gums with the fingers on one side and the thumb on the other, as already described for making a puppy let go. This will make him open his mouth. As he does so, give him the command 'carry', and with the right hand place the dumb-bell in his mouth.

Now you will probably come up against the first obstacle. He will almost certainly try to spit out that nasty lump of wood. It is up to you to see that he doesn't succeed. In the same way as you allowed him to struggle unsuccessfully the first time he was on the leash (until he gave it up as a bad job) you must ensure that he keeps the dumb-bell in his mouth. Not tomorrow or the next day but right now, before you finish the exercise.

Some dogs offer no resistance but others require very firm treatment. Always be very careful not to hurt the teeth or gums as this will cause even more resentment. Keep giving the command 'carry' in a firm tone, holding his jaws shut on the dumb-bell until he stops struggling. Immediately he does so, change your tone of voice and praise him enthusiastically. And take the dumb-bell out of his mouth, giving the command 'drop it'. He may only have given up the struggle to take a breather and if you now try to make him hold the dumb-bell for any length of time, the odds are he will start all over again. If he holds the dumb-bell for a split second until you tell him to 'drop it' you will have gone a step forward. But if you get him to hold it for a minute and then he starts struggling and spits it out when he wants to, you will have gone several steps backwards. Continue like this, making him hold the dumb-bell for gradually longer periods. When he will allow you to place the dumb-bell in his mouth and will hold it for a minute or so without resentment, you have completed the first stage.

The next stage is to get him to take it himself. It is no use to keep opening his mouth and shoving the dumb-bell in indefinitely. Hold it just touching his lips, and, with the fingers and thumb of the left hand in the same position as before, give the command 'carry'. To start with you may have to press the lips very gently, but if you do it properly he should very soon open his mouth in anticipation of your doing so. Very often the first indication that he is going to respond is that he licks the dumb-bell or opens his mouth just a fraction. If he does either, encourage him in a praising tone of voice and he will probably take the dumb-bell, when you must praise him lavishly. It is then a good idea to finish for the day, or at least for that lesson.

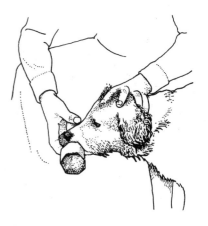

Retrieving Stage 2: Using the left hand to make the dog go forward to the dumb-bell.

Until now the dumb-bell has been going to the dog and the next stage is for the dog to go forward and grasp it. This is done by continuing as before, gradually holding the dumb-bell further and further away from the dog. At first he will stretch his neck to reach it but very soon should have to get up from his sitting position and move forward, which he must be encouraged to do. If he refuses to move forward, you must make him do so by jerking him on the collar, very gently at first, but more severely if necessary. Continue from here until, when you hold the dumb-bell in front of you the dog will, on command, get up from a sitting position beside you, go forward, and take it. When he does this you can move back a step or two and he should bring it to you. So you have now got the dog going forward for an object and bringing it back to you, which is the basis of retrieving.

The next stage can be difficult—getting the dog to pick up the dumb-bell off the ground. Many dogs will take an article quite happily from their handler's hand, even when he holds it on the ground, but take the hand away and they won't touch it. Here, you can encourage the dog by putting the dumb-bell on the ground and as you give the command 'carry' moving it slightly with your hand or even your toe.

If this does not work, you may have to use force. By now your dog should understand the command well. If he cannot be

Retrieving Stage 3: The dog moving forward to pick up the dumb-bell on command. The leash should be slack and is only there to make the dog feel that he is being controlled.

persuaded to pick up the dumb-bell you will have to push his head down and make him pick it up. But this should not prove to be too difficult if you have been working on the right lines. Having made the dog go forward a few steps to pick the dumb-bell off the ground and bring it to you, the rest of this exercise is usually fairly easy. All you have to do is put the dumb-bell further and further forward until the dog will go right out to the end of the leash, pick it up and bring it back. To increase the distance a little move forward a step as he goes forward and take a step back as he comes towards you.

When you can rely on him to do this—not before—take the leash off, throw the dumb-bell about the same distance as you have been using, give the command and your dog should go forward, pick it up, and bring it back. In fact, he should retrieve. Many successful trainers make the dog sit in front, deliver properly and go to heel right from the start but we do not. In teaching any exercise, we concentrate on that one exercise only, and in this case all we are concerned with is getting the dog to retrieve.

You may find that the dog mouths or plays with the dumb-bell when he brings it back to you. If he does, tap him under the chin at the same time scolding him, but not so severely as to make him spit it out. And do not take the dumb-bell from him until he is holding it correctly. Immediately he stops mouthing it, praise him very well, give the command 'drop it' and take it from him. Gradually have him hold it for longer periods until you have a dog that will sit and hold a dumb-bell until you are ready to take it, not until he thinks you should take it.

Many dogs are apt to drop the dumb-bell as you put out your hand to take it. This can be prevented by putting your hand under the dog's chin as though you were going to take the dumb-bell but giving the command 'carry' and making him hold it until he is told to 'drop it'. If he should stop on the retrieve before coming right up to you don't make the common mistake of moving forward to take the dumb-bell. As we have said before, never go towards your dog; always make him come to you.

Having achieved a reliable retrieve, you may now want to speed him up. To do this, make a big effort to praise him very well by voice and actions at the right psychological moments. For example, you throw the dumb-bell, giving the command 'carry' firmly. Your dog walks up to it, not very cheerfully, looks at it then back at you as if to say 'Must I?' You then give an even firmer 'carry' and he opens his mouth to pick it up. If at that moment you say 'carry, carry' very enthusiastically and encouragingly, at the same time running backwards, patting your hands against your thighs he will, more than likely, pick it up and rush back to you with it. If, on the other hand, you just stand and look stupid, he will probably mouth the dumb-bell and come back to you without it, or pick it up and return at a slow walk head and tail down: not what we are aiming for!

If your dog is steady on the sit when you throw his dumb-bell, will hold it for a reasonable length of time and deliver carefully to hand—but not unless—you can speed him up by playing with him. In fact we always finish a retrieving lesson this way. Having got the dog to do a 'serious retrieve', make a great fuss of him and get him really excited. Then just throw the dumb-bell as far as you can, preferably into long grass and let him rush straight off to find it. When he does, run off in the opposite direction so that he will come galloping after you, and take the dumb-bell from him without bothering about the finish.

If you want to have a useful dog, you can teach him to hunt for the dumb-bell and other less conspicuous objects in long grass or other cover. Start by throwing them where he can see them fall but later on hide them when he is out of sight. You can also encourage him to seek back for objects that you have dropped surreptitiously as you walk along. This has some practical value and the dog will enjoy it too. When it comes to sense of smell, the dog has us licked to a standstill, so why not help him to develop it? Not only to develop his scenting ability, but at the same time to develop his instinct to hunt—an instinct that should strengthen with use and make him all the keener to retrieve. Don't start this until the dog is retrieving reliably. Then, when out for a walk, with the dog running ahead of you, preferably on a track or path, drop something obvious, like a handkerchief. Walk a few yards, stop, call the dog back to you and send him back for the object, which he can see. When he retrieves it, make a great fuss of him and continue your walk. Repeat the process but next time walk a little further before

Starting the seekback. *Left*: drop a handkerchief surreptitiously while the dog is running ahead.

Right: Send the dog back to pick up the handkerchief.

sending the dog back. Continue on these lines until you can send the dog back 20 or 30 m (60–100 ft) for an object he can see.

Once your dog shows some enthusiasm for this game, drop the object out of sight—maybe in some tufts of grass beside the path. Call him back to you and if you give him the same command, he should use his nose to find it. It does not require a brilliant dog to do this. When a dog cannot see an object it is as natural for him to use his nose as it is for us to put out a hand to find a light switch in the dark. If you have any trouble it will probably be because the dog is not keen enough on retrieving. Once he will seek back for an object in response to the command to retrieve add another command such as 'seek'. Start with 'seek-carry', changing to 's-e-e-k carry'.

Once the dog finds the object easily, gradually increase the distance until he will seek back quite a long way. Vary the distance you send him back and work on crooked tracks as soon as possible. If a keen dog is always sent back on a straight track of 200–300 m (220–330 yd) he is liable to over-run completely an object left just 25 m (80 ft) in front of him.

Guarding

Like all other instincts, the guarding instinct is handed down from the wild dog. This instinct is not by any means peculiar to the dog, as most of the higher animals will protect their own territory and family. People usually visualize the male as the protector, but the most protective of males has nothing like the ferocity of the female protecting her young. In the domestic dog the guarding instinct is likely to be just as strong in either sex, but it does vary enormously between individuals. In the same litter, it is quite possible to find one dog which is a demon guard, and another that is no use at all. But it is hereditary, and some breeds produce a much higher percentage of good guards than others. And the same applies to different strains within the breeds.

The big problem in choosing a dog which will be a natural guard is that, until he starts to mature, there is no way of knowing whether or not a puppy will have any guarding instinct. Or if he should have, how strong that instinct will be. Some puppies of eight or ten weeks do bark at strangers, but these should be avoided at all costs. At that age a puppy is not protecting his property—because he has not acquired any. He is protecting himself because he is afraid. In other words, he is nervous and will probably grow up into the kind of dog that is liable to bite the wrong people—including members of his own family! But when it comes to the crunch this is just the sort of dog which will hide behind his owner instead of placing himself between his owner and danger.

Which brings us to another problem in choosing a natural guard. Not only is it impossible to assess the guarding instinct in a young puppy, but many people have the wrong ideas about what to look for when they want a dog to protect them. There is a common fallacy that to be any good as a guard, a dog must be constantly barking at every stranger he sees. All the best guards, including the best police dogs, are bold dogs that stand their ground and look a stranger straight in the eye. Some may resent being touched by a stranger but should allow it in the presence of their owners. Many of the best guards will be very friendly towards everyone unless they are protecting their own property. This would be when they are protecting their owners, or when on their own in a house or car.

Of course dogs can be trained to guard and there is an ever increasing demand for such dogs, no doubt due to the ever-increasing thuggery throughout the world. Once a dog has been taught to attack, he cannot be un-trained. He is like a gun with the safety catch released. In some countries it is quite legal for anyone to carry a gun and in these countries a dog trained to attack may be an advantage. In the UK, if anyone enters your premises, with or without permission, and gets bitten you could be heavily fined, while the trespasser would go free. Other countries may have equally ridiculous laws. Generally speaking, it is not advisable for 'the person in the street' to go around with a dog trained to attack. At the same time, there is much you can do to improve the efficiency of your own dog. If he is a natural guard, your number one priority is control. And the best exercise to ensure control is the down. A dog lying down is not going to bite anyone unless they go right up to him.

If your dog does not have a strong guarding instinct it should still be possible to improve him, and at least help him to look the part. And it may surprise you to learn that once again the first essential is control. The overwhelming majority of people who attack others are cowards. It is very seldom that they will put a dog to the test. They will not be afraid of a dog which gambols up to them and licks their hand. However, they will think twice of approaching the same dog if he is lying down between themselves and the owner. Indeed most people are more afraid of a dog which quietly faces them than of one which rushes around barking furiously—quite rightly too.

If your dog tends to rush up to strangers and be friendly with them, make him lie down as he approaches them. Then call him back and make him lie down or stand beside you until the stranger either passes by or comes up to speak to you. This helps to make the dog look the part. Even more important, it helps to strengthen the dog/owner bond, and very often encourages a rather weak guarding instinct.

Some dogs are reluctant to bark when a stranger comes to the door, thereby losing one of the advantages of owning a dog. If the dog tends to bark at anything (i.e. for food) encourage him to do so, gradually teaching him to bark and stop barking on command. Then if someone knocks at the door, simply tell him to bark and very soon he should bark in response to the knock, in anticipation of your command.

Often the easiest way to teach a dog to bark is to encourage him when someone knocks at the door. All too often, the inclination to do so is nipped in the bud by an impatient owner, who tells the dog to be quiet. It is sometimes worth having a friend to help you organize the whole lesson. Obviously you know that someone is going to knock at the door, but it is important that the dog should not know. There are few dogs that will not show some interest when someone knocks. This is when you must do all you can to excite the dog and encourage him to bark. The slightest inclination to utter even a tiny squeak must be praised lavishly. The 'caller' can help by knocking repeatedly, but not continuously, or even by making peculiar noises. As soon as you get the least response praise the dog very well and open the door. The fact that the dog knows the caller does not matter. At this stage you are trying to teach the dog to bark in response to a knock at the door.

If a dog is over-friendly or over-aggressive, put him on a leash before opening the door to a caller.

But once the dog starts to bark the problem may be reversed—he won't stop! The dog that won't stop barking is a more common problem than one that refuses to bark. And nothing is more infuriating than standing on the doorstep trying to carry out a conversation with someone whose dog is barking incessantly.

Once again we come back to the down exercise. Before you open the door, make the dog lie down in a strategic position behind it. Stop him barking before you open the door. If necessary, put him on a leash so that you can correct him with the slip collar. A friend, the other side of the door, who knows what you are doing will be a help.

A dog lying down won't attack the caller when the door is

Far left: The dog is in the correct position for maximum protection.

Left: A dog in this position is useless as a guard, as an attacker could easily rush through the door and shut the dog out.

opened, nor, if he is over-friendly will he leap all over him or her. But most important of all, the person standing on the doorstep will not know whether the dog is friendly or aggressive. If the dog has any guarding instinct the above procedure will help to develop it. Once the person has been accepted and asked to come in, the dog can be encouraged to be friendly towards that person. Because of the pack instinct, most dogs instinctively want to take part in their leader's activities. If you encourage him to bark behind the door, then put him down quietly before you open it, he will almost certainly watch the person on the doorstep. And this is all that is needed to make the majority of wrongdoers change their minds. This is in contrast to the dog which rushes outside and barks furiously behind the caller making it easy for him to barge in and shut the door in the dog's face.

Next to the hunting instinct, the guarding instinct is probably the most useful to man. But this great asset can be, and all too often is, a great liability. There is obviously the over-aggressive dog, with which we have dealt. Much more common is the dog which guards its own property against his owner. Almost invariably this situation arises when a submissive owner acquires a dominant dog. And it is amazing how much domination some owners will accept from their dogs!

Very often the trouble starts with quite a young puppy, which growls or bares his teeth when the owner tries to take away his bone or toy. Some owners think this very funny—a sign that the puppy 'has guts'. Others say, 'Oh well, it's only natural', and let the puppy keep his bone. But the pup has more sense than either and says to himself, 'The stupid great twit is afraid of me. I'll soon be the boss!' And very often he soon is the boss. By allowing this sort of behaviour the owner completely destroys the leader/follower relationship at the very time he or she should be trying to develop it.

It is interesting to note that dominant or quick-tempered people never have this problem. When challenged by the puppy, their immediate reflex action is to strike back, just like the bitch with her puppies. 'But', some people say, 'I don't want to be nasty to him. I want him to like me.' Nonetheless, the first essential is that the dog should respect his master. And dogs that respect their masters nearly always like them better than those that don't.

The big problem about this type of behaviour is that it rapidly, very rapidly, gets worse. All young animals gain confidence as they become older. In the case of the possessive dog, the stage will quickly be reached where the dog takes possession of anything he fancies, which very often includes the best chair. He also becomes more difficult to train, partly

Some people think it funny when a puppy guards his food, but it almost invariably leads to trouble later and should be checked when it first happens. Simply hold the puppy by the scruff with one hand and remove the food with the other. When he settles down and shows some respect for his master, give him the food back.

because aggression has been allowed to develop, and partly because the dog grows bigger, stronger and more dangerous.

Like all unwanted traits this is one that should be quickly nipped in the bud. When your puppy is feeding pick up his dish. He may not resent it at all, in which case just stroke him, tell him what a good boy he is and give it back to him. But be ready for any sign of aggression. If he shows the least sign of resentment take hold of him by the scruff with one hand, remove the dish with the other and at the same time scold him by tone of voice. If he continues to resent this, give him a good shake until he settles down. As soon as he does, praise him and let him have his food back. Repeat these tactics every time you feed him until he will allow you to pick up his food without resentment.

If the pup is really aggressive and attempts to attack your hand, don't give him time to do so. Strike him right across the face with the back of the hand he tried to bite. The object is not so much to hurt, as to frighten the puppy. And don't be afraid to frighten him. This type of puppy won't be put off for very long. Of course, you must be nice to him as soon as he gives up being possessive—even if he did nip your finger in the process!

6 General care

Grooming

All dogs, from tiny smooth Chihuahuas to giant St Bernards, need grooming. In the wild, dogs clean each other's coats in an act of friendship and this contributes to the social life of the whole pack. So a grooming session, which should never be turned into a battle, strengthens the bond between dog and owner when properly carried out. It also makes the dog more pleasant to live with, makes him feel good, helps to keep the coat and skin healthy, gets rid of loose hairs and dirt and tones up the muscles.

Puppies seldom need much grooming, but they should be accustomed to it at an early age. It is worth spending some time on this as a dog that will stand or lie down quietly to be groomed will behave much more sensibly when examined by a show judge or veterinary surgeon. Nearly all puppies enjoy being talked to and fondled. So when you have a few minutes to spare pick up the pup and hold him on your lap for a short while. Or, if you have a very large puppy, sit on the floor with him. Quietly coax him to keep still while you run your hands over his coat, open his mouth, look inside his ears, pick up his feet, and so on. To begin with, he will probably wriggle all over the place. Hold him gently but firmly, talk to him all the time, keep the session short and he should learn what is wanted. Gradually increase the time you keep him still, and start brushing with a soft brush. Progress to having him on a table, keep him standing by supporting his tummy with one hand while brushing with the other. Vary this by carefully pushing him into a sitting or lying position, making sure he stays there, if only for a few seconds. Never frighten the pup, spend time getting him to relax, always finish on a good note and be lavish with your praise.

Another useful position, especially for Poodles and long-coated breeds, is lying flat on the side. Once the pup will stay lying down quietly, gently roll him over on his side. Just keep him there for a minute or so rubbing his tummy, which most

Teach your dog to keep still when you are grooming him. He should learn to stay in whatever position you want. Sitting, as shown here, is probably best when you are brushing his chest.

dogs enjoy, and tell him how good he is. Once he is happy and relaxed in this position, start brushing out his coat.

A few minutes grooming every day and a thorough going-over once a week keeps most breeds in good order. But unless you are really keen on grooming, don't forget that breeds such as Afghans, Old English Sheepdogs, Pekingese and the like need a considerable time spent on them every day. Basically you will need a good quality brush and a steel comb. Very short-coated breeds will only need a stiff brush and possibly a hound glove or mitt. These can be of rubber, short wire or bristle, or corduroy velvet. Used with plenty of pressure, they will help get rid of dead coat and stimulate the skin. Short-coated dogs can be given a final polish either with the bare hands, a chamois leather or a piece of silk.

When brushing the body coat, use long firm strokes which will tone up the muscles as well as clean the hair.

Combs should always be used sparingly, a long silky coat can be ruined by too much tearing and pulling with a comb. Brush a little of the coat at a time, gradually working over the whole animal, make sure the bristles go right down to the skin. And while you are brushing, check to see that the dog does not have fleas or any other unwanted visitors. Fleas are very small—and active—and jump. If the dog is scratching and you suspect fleas, there will most likely be masses of little black specks in the coat, which are flea droppings. A medicated shampoo is a very good way of clearing fleas, but if you don't want to bath the dog there are a number of suitable sprays and dusting powders that can be used instead.

Unfortunately, the fleas will not only be on the dog but in the house too. Fleas simply love close-carpeted, centrally heated houses! So dust around the dog's bed and the carpet and then vacuum carefully. Also wash the dog's bedding. Flea collars are useful too. These are impregnated plastic collars, which allow a slow release of insecticide. Some dogs are allergic to them, but might tolerate a flea tag which would not be in such close contact with the skin.

Other common parasites which might be found when brushing the coat are ticks and lice. Dogs seldom get infested with large numbers of ticks and a few can be removed by hand. This is easiest when the ticks are gorged with blood. Grasp the tick between finger and thumb and squeeze it out with the thumb nail. If you are doubtful of your skill and worried about leaving the head behind, dab the tick with a bit of cotton wool soaked in surgical spirit—or gin if that is all you have around! That will make it loose its hold on the skin. It is difficult to stop dogs picking up ticks in the countryside, although regular dusting with insecticidal powder helps.

Lice can be seen in the coat as small grey creatures that cling firmly to the hairs and do not hop about like fleas. They lay their eggs on the hairs and these look rather like specks of scurf. A medicated shampoo is the best treatment, again not forgetting the bedding. As the eggs will hatch out at a later date the dog will need another bath in ten or fourteen days time.

When brushing the coat, make a careful check behind the ears, under the tail and between the pads—all places where mats tend to form. If not too bad, these can often be teased out with the fingers and then carefully combed.

Wire-haired dogs, such as Wire Fox Terriers, should have a hard outer coat and thick soft undercoat and require regular stripping. This is done with a stripping knife rather like a penknife with a serrated edge. All the Terrier breeds are trimmed differently, but there is no reason why you should not learn to do this yourself if you want to. Try to get a breeder to give you some lessons, and/or buy a specialist book on your own breed. For normal everyday grooming, this type of coat generally needs a good brushing.

Pomeranians, Chows, Keeshonds and all breeds with stiff, stand-off coats should have their coats brushed against the growth of the hair first and then carefully brushed back into place. When these breeds shed their thick undercoats, a special rake can be helpful in loosening the dead hair.

Poodles do not shed their coats—they just keep growing them. To keep them looking smart, regular clipping is necessary. This is done at most beauty parlours and canine beautician shops. But if you are content with a 'short back and sides', such as a lamb clip, it is not too difficult to do it yourself. You will need clippers, sharp hairdressing scissors, brush and comb and a pair of scissors with curved blades and blunt ends. There are a number of books explaining the various clips in detail, but some expert tuition would be worthwhile.

Don't forget to keep all brushes, combs, scissors, and so on clean. It is no use trying to keep your dog clean with dirty equipment.

Make it a routine job to check the following points at least once a week. Make sure you allow enough time to go over the dog properly. Start at the head end and have a look at the eyes. These should be bright, clear and free from discharge. Dogs with either very deep-set or protruding eyes sometimes suffer from slightly sore eyes because of dust or ash getting into them. Washing out the eye with normal saline solution should ease the irritation. Normal saline solution can be made by adding a teaspoonful of salt to $\frac{1}{2}$ litre (1 pt) of boiled water and allowing it to cool. Apart from this, never treat eyes with anything else unless it has been approved by your veterinary surgeon. Eyes are very delicate, and if any trouble does not clear up rapidly see your veterinary surgeon at once.

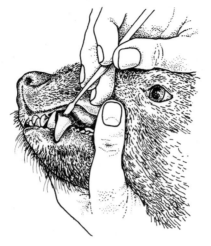

Teeth can be kept free from plaque quite easily, but tartar deposits need to be removed before they damage teeth and gums. With a little practice, this can be done with a tooth scaler as shown. Push the gum well back to make sure that you scrape only the teeth and do not damage the gum.

Now check the dog's nose, which should be clear and free from discharge. In very hot or very cold weather noses can become sore and cracked. A little olive or cod liver oil rubbed into the nose will help. The dog will soon lick most of it off, but it won't harm him and what is left will help the sore nose.

Open the mouth and check the teeth and gums. Dogs, like humans, collect tartar on their teeth, and it does them no good either. It causes bad breath, gum disease and loose teeth. If the dog is given a certain amount of dry food and hard biscuits, this will help to prevent tartar forming. Chewing on large marrow bones, rawhide chews and large, hard rubber balls will all help to keep the teeth clean. If you want to clean the dog's teeth you can use a toothbrush and toothpaste, or just rub round the teeth and gums with some gauze soaked in saline solution or bicarbonate of soda solution. Small breeds seem to be more prone to teeth troubles than some of the larger ones. Prevention is better than cure, so try not to let the teeth get into a bad state, or if you feel you are fighting a losing battle consult your veterinary surgeon. If the tartar deposit is bad, the teeth will have to be scaled. If your dog is quiet to handle you can learn to do this yourself with a tooth scaler. Be very gentle and work from the root downwards, doing a little at a time.

Lastly at the head end are the ears. Like eyes, ears are delicate, and you should never prod or poke into a dog's ear. Lift the earflap and see if the inside is clean, free from discharge and smell. Most ears get dirty, but a wipe round with a piece of damp cotton wool should clean off any surface dirt. If there seems some slight irritation, but you can see no cause for it, pour a little warm olive oil into the ear, which should float out any specks of dirt or dust causing trouble. Some dogs grow tufts of hair in the ear canal which, if excessive, can become stuck up with wax and eventually block the canal. It can easily

Ears are delicate organs and care should be taken to keep them clean. Wipe round very gently and never poke into the ear canal.

If the dog has been used to having his nails cut from puppyhood, he should sit quite happily while this is done.

When clipping nails, be careful not to cut the sensitive quick. It is better to take off too little than too much.

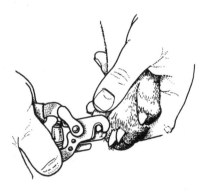

be cleared out by grasping the hair with finger and thumb, or tweezers, and giving a sharp jerk. Do a little at a time and don't pull. A dog's ears are very sensitive. Check for tangles behind the ears, and in breeds such as Spaniels make sure the edges of the earflap are clean and healthy. Because the ears get dragged along the ground they sometimes pick up grass seeds, mud or thorns and become quite sore. Carefully brush and comb the hair out and if necessary wash, dry well and apply a little antiseptic ointment.

Now work down towards the feet. Look at the pads for cracks or small cuts. Town dogs can get cracked pads from too much walking on hard concrete. A little olive oil will soothe them if not too bad. Or the dog can wear a special boot for a few days. Look between the pads for matted hair. If formed, these mats collect grit and dirt which in turn leads to very sore feet. Cut the mats out carefully with a pair of blunt-ended, curved scissors. Wash the feet and dust with a little antiseptic powder.

When a dog is standing naturally, the nails should just touch the ground. Very long nails make a dog move badly, are uncomfortable for him and cause the foot to spread. Some dogs' nails never seem to need clipping but others, especially those exercised on soft ground, may require regular trimming. Nail clippers can be bought at most pet shops, and, as with other equipment it pays to purchase a good-quality pair. They will last longer and make the job easier. A coarse nail file can be used for filing off the rough edges. Many dogs that dislike having their nails cut have no objection to filing. In light-coloured nails the quick is usually visible as a small pink line running down the nail. Be careful not to cut this as it will bleed profusely and be very painful for the dog. If your dog has both light and dark nails start cutting the light ones first then cut the others to the same length. If they are all dark, clip off very little at first until you are sure how far the quick reaches. It is fairly safe to trim off the tip of the nail where it starts to turn downwards. Finish the nails off with the file. Don't forget the dew claws (if these have not been removed), found on the inside of the leg a little way up from the foot. As they do not touch the ground they never get worn down, and if not clipped keep on growing. If neglected they can grow right into the flesh and cause a bad abscess.

If you own a male dog, examine his sheath and the area round it. Most male dogs have a small amount of light-coloured discharge from the end of the prepuce, which is generally considered normal. If there is a smelly or discoloured discharge consult your veterinary surgeon. But apart from normal discharge, every time the dog cocks his leg he leaves a few drops of urine scattered around underneath. So it makes him pleasanter to live with if the long hairs on, and around the sheath are kept trimmed short and occasionally washed with warm water and mild soap.

Just underneath and to either side of the root of the tail are two small glands called anal sacs. Wild dogs on a diet of whole small animals including hair, bones, fur and so on usually have no trouble emptying these glands when they defecate. But few dogs today eat such a diet, and the soft types of diets allow the sacs to fill up with an evil-smelling liquid. If you notice the dog rubbing his bottom along the ground or licking his anus excessively that is probably the reason why. If the sacs are emptied at this stage all should be well. But if neglected they become impacted and a nasty abscess can form. The remedy is to empty them. Hold up the tail, place a large pad of cotton wool or tissue over the anus, place your finger and thumb on either side of the glands and press firmly. Or you can do one at a time by inserting one finger in the anus and squeezing the gland between finger and thumb. Try to persuade your veterinary surgeon to show you how to do this; if you don't fancy it much, ask him to do it for you.

Bathing

Nobody likes a dirty dog around the house, so the answer to the question 'How often should I bath my dog?' is, whenever he needs it. If he looks dirty and smells dirty then bath him. As with general grooming, accustom your puppy to baths when he is quite small and you will have far less trouble when he is a great big dog. When bathing puppies, always pick a warm day and make sure the pup is well dried afterwards. Unless using a special flea shampoo use a good dog shampoo, not just any old detergent out of the kitchen sink. Use warm, not hot, water. Put a little water in the bath, sink, whatever you are using, depending on the size of the dog; if the bottom is slippery put a rubber mat down for the dog to stand on. Pour on the shampoo and work up a good lather, rubbing it well into the coat. Leave the head until last. Once a dog has his head wet he will try to shake, and probably succeed, which you may not care for half way through the bath. Be careful not to get any shampoo into the eyes and ears. If you have a fidgety dog, it is a good idea to plug his ears with a large wad of cotton wool to keep out the soap suds. Once he is well washed, pour warm water over him to rinse the coat thoroughly. Make sure you rinse out all the shampoo. Slip a lead on and let him out for a good shake. Don't let him run loose at this stage—if inside he will head for the best carpet and if outside for the muddiest patch he can find. Mop off the surplus water with a rough towel, rubbing briskly if the dog is short or wire coated. With long-coated breeds, it is best to mop up as much of the moisture as possible and finish with a hair dryer, gently combing out the hair as it dries. This will prevent tangles and ensure that the coat lies correctly when dry. Having said all that, if you have a short-coated dog or a very large one, it might well be easier, and will not harm the dog, if you take him outside on a really warm day and wash him with the garden hose and let him run around in the sun to dry. But don't do this with an Afghan you intend to show on the following day!

Beds and bedding

Once the pup has stopped growing, you can finally decide on what type of bed he is to have. Pet shops are full of the most luxurious beds and baskets. However, baskets are not the best type of bed. They are draughty, collect dust and dirt and unless supplied with a good thick blanket, are not too comfortable. Bean bag beds are popular with dogs and owners, and are convenient to throw in the back of the car when the dog is travelling. Whichever type you choose, make sure it is large enough to allow the dog to stretch out fully, is warm and washable. Never put a dog to bed wet; give him a good rub down first. Be careful where you place the bed. If the dog has spent the evening in front of the fire, it won't do him much good if he then has to go to bed in the hall with a howling gale blowing under the front door. Old dogs often feel the cold and may suffer from rheumatism, so make extra sure they go to bed warm and dry. The small heated pad recommended for puppies can be very useful for old dogs.

Feeding

By the time your puppy is about twelve months old he will only need one, or at the most two meals a day. Feed him whenever it is most convenient for you. The dog won't mind when it is, as long as he gets it!

We once believed in the importance of regular feeding. However, when we started giving demonstrations, and working our dogs in films, it became quite impossible to feed regularly. For over thirty years, we have fed the dogs when there is time to feed them, and frequently miss a day altogether. If anything, the dogs seem to be better for it. This is not surprising when one considers the feeding habits of the wild dog, which never knows when or where his next meal will appear.

Fortunately for us, the dog is a most accommodating and adaptable creature. The wild dog feeds at very irregular intervals, eating even more irregular quantities of food, but the domestic dog appears to be quite happy eating the same food at the same time every day. In the majority of households it is more convenient to feed the dog at the same time every day, although there is no need to give him the same food every time.

Never feed immediately before or after exercise or before a journey. If you buy an adult dog, keep to the type of food and feeding time he has been used to until he has settled down. Then, if you want to change, do it gradually. Your friends will be full of good advice about feeding, and will all have different ideas. As long as the dog has a balanced diet, is fit and well, it doesn't much matter what he is having—it obviously suits him! There are innumerable complete commercial diets available now. Most of the better quality ones are very good and usually have an analysis of the contents on the can or packet. If you feed a complete diet, don't upset things by buying all the many additives that are advertised. The dog won't need them. An excess or imbalance of various minerals and vitamins can cause as much, if not more damage to a dog's health than a slight lack of them.

If you feed a dry food, always have fresh water available. Many of the foods found in most kitchens have useful feeding value and can all be used to vary the dog's diet. Eggs, cheese, milk, cereals, baked wholemeal bread, cooked vegetables, milk puddings are all good. Dogs in hard work, such as gundogs, need more food and extra protein to make up the extra energy used. Old dogs need to be treated more like puppies, and often do better on two or three small meals rather than one large one. They usually need extra calcium and fewer calories to keep fit.

Avoid giving titbits except on special occasions, and never feed a dog when you are having a meal yourself. If you can't stop the family feeding him at mealtimes, banish him from the room while you are eating. Try to prevent your dog from becoming too fat. This can be very difficult, especially in some breeds, but once a dog has put on fat, it is very difficult to get it off again and very hard on the dog. Many owners kill their dogs by giving them too much to eat, so have as your motto, 'fit not fat'.

7 Health and first aid

Worming

You may try to avoid the subject—but you can't! Sooner or later your dog, and everyone else's dog, will have worms of one type or another. The general public has been warned—over-warned some would say—through the media, of the dangers to humans from dogs which have worms. The majority of doctors and veterinary surgeons would agree that there is a risk, but most feel that it is only a slight one. Even so, that is as good a reason as any for strict control of worms in your dog.

A few worms probably do the dog little harm, but he should certainly be wormed regularly. The most common types found are roundworms (usually in puppies and young adults) and tapeworms. Roundworms can be seen when they pass out with the droppings. They are whitish in colour, threadlike, and 5–15 cm (2–6 in) long. They can cause vomiting or diarrhoea in puppies, but older dogs may show few, if any, symptoms. Tapeworms are seen as small flat segments $\frac{1}{2}$–1 cm ($\frac{1}{5}$–$\frac{2}{5}$ in) long, usually sticking to the hair round the anus or wriggling about on fresh droppings. If you think your dog has worms, take a sample of the faeces to your veterinary surgeon for examination, he will then be able to prescribe the correct dose for the type of worm with which your dog is infected. When you worm your dog, also make sure he has no fleas as these form part of the life cycle of certain worms. Dogs can become infected with tapeworms from eating raw meat and offal from sheep, cows or pigs, and in some countries it is illegal to feed raw meat to dogs. There are many other types of worms, such as whip worms, heartworms, hookworms, stomach worms. All are difficult to diagnose and need professional treatment. Don't panic about worms, they have been around for a very long time. Modern medicines are effective and simple to administer, and with sensible precautions worms should cause no problems to your family or your dog.

Vaccinations

Although your puppy may have had all the necessary vaccinations, he will need booster doses. How often these are needed depends on various circumstances and you should be advised by your vet about it. Few boarding kennels will accept dogs without an up-to-date vaccination certificate for hardpad, distemper, leptospirosis and parvo virus. Rabies vaccination is required by law in many countries where rabies outbreaks occur. Dogs, generally speaking, are resistant to tetanus, but it does occur, usually in country districts. Although it is not usual to vaccinate against it, it can be done by the vet should it be considered necessary.

Basic nursing

There usually comes a time when even the healthiest dog needs a dose of medicine or a pill, has to have an operation or needs to have a wound treated and bandaged. If the dog is already ill, it will only make matters worse if you have to fight and struggle to force his medicine down his throat. Far better to get him used to taking liquid medicine and pills when he is still a puppy and treating it as a game. Use chocolate drops or small round dog candies, something that tastes good. Give the pup one or two to eat then place your hand over his muzzle, lift his head up slightly, pull the lips down over the top teeth and press inwards, keeping the lips between the fingers and teeth. This will cause him to open his mouth. Be very gentle and talk to the pup all the time. If the puppy is small, pop the pill right at the back of the tongue, shut the mouth and massage the throat until the pill is swallowed. It is a good idea at this stage to let him have another one to eat. Done this way most dogs will almost enjoy being dosed!

If the pup is a large one, open the mouth the same way but hold the pill between two fingers and thumb and push it well down the throat with the fingers. If there is real reluctance to

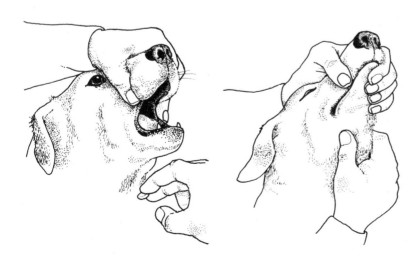

To give a pill open the dog's mouth as shown, keeping the upper lips round the top teeth. Push the pill well back over the tongue. Then shut the dog's mouth, tilt the head slightly upwards and gently massage the throat until the pill is swallowed.

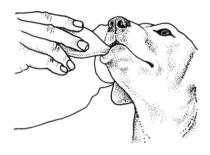

Liquid medicine is more easily given from a small bottle than from a spoon. Pour the liquid steadily and slowly into a pouch formed by pulling the side of the cheek outwards.

swallow, hold the nostrils shut for a few seconds. This is often enough to make the dog take a gulp of air which in turn will cause him to swallow. Don't mix tablets with food. The food can get spilt, or the dog may only eat a portion of it, and then you have no idea how much medicine has been taken.

Liquid medicine is best given with the dog (or puppy) sitting, and someone holding him still. Again use something palatable such as milk or gravy. Although a spoon can be used many people find a small bottle or syringe—minus the needle of course—easier to manage. Gently insert a finger between the teeth and cheek. Pull the lip outwards until a pouch is formed. Keep the head steady and slowly pour a little liquid into the pouch. The head should be tilted upwards very slightly. Wait until the liquid is swallowed before pouring in a little more. Never pour much at a time as it could cause choking.

One of the first things a vet will ask you if you report that your dog is not well is whether he has a temperature. The temperature should be taken in the rectum, a normal reading being 38.61°C (101.5°F). Use a snub-nosed thermometer, and put a little petroleum jelly or oil on the end. Hold up the tail with one hand and insert the thermometer gently into the rectum with the other. Hold it there for the required time, wipe it and read it. And don't forget to shake the mercury down again or you might give yourself a nasty fright next time you take his temperature! Hold the thermometer firmly when it is in the rectum as some dogs can manage to draw it right inside!

Some dogs insist on tearing off bandages, pulling out stitches or scratching at an injured ear, in which case it is best to put on an 'Elizabethan collar'. This can be made out of a circle of strong cardboard with a hole in the centre. Make a slit in the cardboard, put it round the dog's neck and lace it up. A plastic bucket is also useful; cut a hole in the bottom, large enough to go over the dog's head. If the edges of the hole are not smooth, pad them to make it more comfortable.

A dog's temperature is more easily taken when he is standing. Gently push the lubricated thermometer into the rectum and hold there for a couple of minutes.

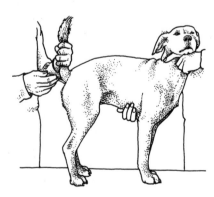

A dog returning from the surgery after an operation, or convalescing after a severe illness, will want careful nursing. He must be kept warm and dry in a well-ventilated room. The heated pad suggested for puppies is useful, or a well wrapped-up, not too hot, hot water bottle can be used instead. By all means coax the patient to eat but never force food on him. Soft, easily digested foods given in small amounts are best. Make sure the dog gets some peace and quiet. Much as the family might love to pop in to see how he is, it will do him more good to sleep and rest. Never forget to groom a sick dog and keep him clean. A dirty, unkempt dog quickly loses interest in everything. Always have fresh water available. Once he is up and about, don't overdo the exercise. Build up his strength gradually and make sure he doesn't get wet and cold during this time.

It is always advisable to contact your veterinary surgeon in good time. Some illnesses treated properly at the onset can be cured quickly, but if left for a few days might well prove fatal. Even so, some things are emergencies and others not. Your vet won't thank you for getting him out of a warm bed at 1 am just because the dog is scratching his ear!

Very severe vomiting, continuing for an hour or two, is definitely a case for the vet—and don't give the dog anything before you take him there. The same for severe diarrhoea, which does not stop within twenty-four hours. And finally, if you are unsure about what is wrong, please do not treat your dog with some pills left over from the last visit to the vet. Or, even worse, something that Dad had from the doctor when he had stomach cramp. Treatment without proper diagnosis is stupid, uncaring and dangerous.

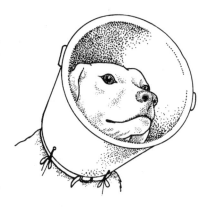

Elizabethan collars, as shown, can be made quite simply from stiff cardboard or a plastic bucket. Although not too popular with the wearer, they can be a great help to stop dogs from scratching at sore ears, stitches and so on.

First aid

It is a good idea to have at least some knowledge of first aid for the more common accidents that may occur. First aid can be defined as essential emergency treatment to help the casualty until he can be treated by a qualified person. With even a little knowledge, you are far less likely to panic than if you have no idea what to do.

Drowning Most dogs love swimming, but many have drowned because they could not climb up an overhanging embankment or concrete wall. Puppies can fall into the goldfish pond, and even strong swimmers can fight a losing battle against a strong tide. Having got the dog out of the water, lift him by the hind legs and let him swing to allow the water in his lungs to drain out. Then pull out his tongue, make sure his breathing is not obstructed, and if he is unconscious begin artificial respiration. For this, place him on his right side, put your hands over the heart area, press firmly then release and repeat. Mouth-to-mouth respiration can be used, but make sure the dog's mouth is shut, cover the dog's nose with your mouth and force air in through the nose.

Burns Whenever possible, burns should be treated by immersion in cold water for at least twenty minutes. If it is not possible to immerse the burnt area, treat it with ice packs or pour water over the burn until veterinary help can be obtained.

Poisoning If you know the dog has eaten poison, try to induce him to vomit immediately. A small piece of washing soda pushed down the throat, salt or mustard and water can be used. Then take the dog as fast as you can to the vet, taking a sample of the poison with you. If you suspect poisoning, but don't know what it is and the dog is already vomiting, don't give any treatment, just rush him to the vet.

Heat stroke In very hot climates dogs can quite frequently suffer from heat stroke, but the most common cause is leaving a dog in a closed car. In relatively warm weather the temperature in a closed car can rise quickly to 37 or 38°C (100°F). Sensible, caring owners *never* leave dogs shut up in closed cars. A dog suffering from heat stroke will be panting, have a fast pulse, reddened eyes and gums, a high temperature and may vomit. If these signs are evident, he needs treatment fast before he lapses into a coma. If you can get the dog to a bath, place him in a bath full of cold water. If not, try to find a hose and run water over him. In fact, find any source of water you can. Once the dog starts to recover, dry him off, keep him cool and encourage him to drink. If recovery is not complete and fairly rapid, take him to the vet for a check up.

Traffic accidents Unfortunately, these are far too common, and your knowledge of first aid is more likely to be needed for these than for any other situation. The dog will probably be suffering from shock, frightened and in pain, so he may well bite; yes, even his owner. Firstly, put an emergency muzzle on him. You will not be able to help the dog if he takes a chunk out of your hand. For this, you need a length of any strong pliable material: a belt, tie, crepe bandage, scarf, anything handy. Form a loop, slip it over the dog's nose, pull it tight under the chin, take both

Every dog owner should know how to apply an effective emergency muzzle. Form a loop from a bandage, tie or whatever is available. Slip it over the dog's muzzle, tie it under the chin and pass the ends behind the ears and tie them in a bow.

ends back behind the ears and tie them firmly. If unconscious, make sure the dog can breathe and has no obstruction in his mouth, and move him as little as possible. Check any wounds to see that there is no foreign body there, then apply a pressure bandage. Any clean material, such as handkerchiefs, can be used. Make a pad, place it over the wound and bandage firmly. Don't remove it if the blood seeps through. Bandage again on top until you can get the patient to a vet. If you have to move an injured dog, find a makeshift stretcher or use the car rug. Slide the rug under the dog, have a person at each end and lift him carefully into the car. A dog with internal injuries may show no outward signs, but will be breathing fast with a rapid pulse and clammy skin. This needs immediate veterinary treatment. An injured dog may struggle very violently and require quite some effort to restrain him. Handle him firmly but gently and if he is conscious talk to him soothingly in an effort to calm him down.

Dogs seriously injured in motor accidents should be moved as little as possible. But if necessary a car rug makes a suitable emergency stretcher. Be sure that the dog is lying comfortably. The hind legs should be placed carefully beside each other.

Choking One of the most usual causes of choking is a small rubber ball—which the dog should never have been allowed to have. A ball stuck in the throat will, at the best, cause considerable distress and, at the worst, choke the dog to death. If still breathing, he may need an anaesthetic before the ball can be dislodged.

Dogs can also get pieces of stick wedged in the mouth, and although they do not cause choking, some dogs get in a complete panic, scrabbling and tearing at the mouth. Find someone to help restrain the dog. Wedge the mouth open (you will almost certainly get bitten otherwise) and lever the obstruction out.

8 Play and exercise

Tricks

Most dogs enjoy 'showing off' and one way of letting them enjoy this is to teach them a few tricks. It can also prove useful in another way. If a timid dog is taught to shake hands and to perform a few other simple tricks, it will give him confidence when meeting strange people.

So let us start with 'shaking hands'. In fact, this is a natural action. All small puppies instinctively knead at their mother's breasts to stimulate the flow of milk. When the pups are a little older, the bitch often stands for them to suckle and they sit underneath reaching up at her with their paws. If your puppy wants to shake hands with you encourage him to do so, giving him a definite command each time. He will very soon realize what is wanted and you will feel very smug thinking how easy he is going to be to train! Maybe!

With an older dog the two usual methods are as follows. Place the dog in a sitting position, tap under the foreleg saying 'shake' and when he lifts his paw take hold of it and praise him well. Repeat this until you can do without the tap and just hold out your hand and give the command. The other method is to have the dog sitting, give the command and press his right shoulder with your left hand (or vice versa). This should make him lift his paw off the ground, when you promptly take hold of it and praise him. Gradually ease off the pressure until he does it when you hold out your hand and tell him to 'shake'.

With 'shaking hands' and 'begging', which we will deal with next, make very sure that the dog only does it when told to, as nothing is worse than a dog which keeps poking at you with his paw, probably muddy, or sits up begging every time you eat something.

Don't teach your puppy to sit up and beg too young, as it can put strain on an undeveloped back. Small, stocky dogs usually find this an easy trick to learn, but larger breeds with spindly legs can have difficulty finding the right balance. With a small dog, all that is usually needed is to sit the dog, tell him to 'beg' and hold a titbit above his head and encourage him to sit up. If

A dog that is reluctant to 'shake hands' can often be encouraged by pressing on the shoulder to make him lift his paw.

this does not work treat him as you would a larger dog. In this case, put the dog on a collar and leash and sit him in a corner of a room. This will give support to his back when he tries to sit up. Tell him to 'beg', gently pull up on the leash, at the same time lifting up his front paws with your other hand. Try to get him properly balanced and reward him with a titbit. Once he sits up readily in the corner try him away from any support but be ready to steady him if he wobbles. It may take time, but with patience and encouragement most dogs can manage eventually.

Some dogs are naturals at catching anything thrown to them, and others take a while to see what is wanted. If you have one of the former all you need to do is teach him to catch on command. The other sort have to be taught from scratch. Have the dog on a collar and leash and have a supply of titbits in your pocket. Have a titbit in your free hand, get the dog's attention, tell him to 'catch' and from a short distance, very gently toss him a titbit. If he misses stop him picking it up and grab it before he can. Keep trying until he manages a catch and then stop for the day. If you think you are going to be there all day without a catch, move in very close and just drop the titbit into his mouth. Then start again the next day. This can need great patience, but usually the dog suddenly gets the hang of it and there is no more trouble. Once he has been taught to catch you can use a ball and let him jump in the air to catch it—very good exercise. But make sure you use a large, soft ball and never throw it too hard.

Once your dog lies down on command he can be taught to 'die for his country'. First, teach him to lie on his side (if he does not already do so). When he is lying down pull the lead tight on the side on which you want him to lie at the same time pushing him over with the other hand on his shoulder. Some dogs fight against this and need plenty of reassurance. Once he knows the command and is lying flat without needing to be pulled or pushed into position, all that is needed then is to scold him in a very harsh tone if he moves his eyes, ears, tail, or anything else, telling him 'dead dog' or whatever words you are going to use. Again the dog may be a little confused, so make a great fuss of him when he is doing it right. To make this trick really impressive, the dog needs to drop straight down in one go. So start with him standing on a leash. Tell him 'down', and give a jerk on the leash for extra reinforcement. Then tell him to lie on his side and finally to play dead. Speed this up until he goes straight down for the last command only.

The next one is not to be recommended for huge dogs with fragile owners! Small dogs can easily be taught to jump up into their owner's arms and treat it as a great game. Squat down, have the dog in front of you and give him the command you are going to use; clap your hands and using a very excited voice try

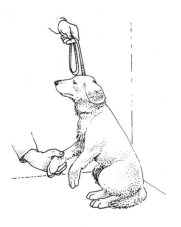

Sometimes long-legged dogs have trouble balancing when learning to beg. It will help if you start with the dog sitting in a corner of the room and support him with the leash. Lift his front paws in your hand until he can balance alone.

to encourage him to climb onto your knees. Then try to have him jumping onto them. Next, stand up, but with your knees bent and hold your hands low ready to catch him when he launches himself at you. Finally, stand straight up and have him jump right up into your arms.

Teaching a dog to 'speak' on command is not really a trick, as it has many practical uses, apart from being one of the tests in obedience trials. For this, you need to study your dog and find out what makes him bark. Sometimes it will be when he is first let out, when he wants his dinner, when you pick up his lead, when someone knocks at the door. If you are unlucky enough not to be able to find anything try teasing him with some food, or tying him up and running away. Whenever he does bark, rush back and praise him well and try to have him do it again. Once the dog is barking reliably on command teach him to stop. The easiest way to stop a noisy dog barking is to teach it to bark on command—and then teach it to stop!

Swimming

Contrary to general belief, not all dogs can swim. We owned a Greyhound and a friend a Boxer, and neither dog could, or would swim. Once they were in deep water they simply let themselves sink and never even struggled. So if you have that sort, forget the swimming! However, the majority of dogs love swimming and it is excellent exercise. Some dogs just splash around in a stream, venture in deeper and find they are swimming. If a dog is keen on retrieving he will usually go straight into water to fetch his ball or a stick. But don't throw a stick into deep water the first time. If the dog has never been in water before, he could be put off for life. Choose a lake, shallow river or seashore with a gently shelving beach. If the dog goes in happily, gradually increase the distance you throw the object until he is actually swimming.

With a non-retriever that is not too keen to go in, you will need time and patience. One way is to go in the water yourself and call the dog to you. If you have a small dog you will only need to paddle but with a large breed you will have to choose a warm day and take to swimming yourself! Another way to start, is to go out with a dog that already swims and which is friendly with your dog. If the one goes in the other will more than likely follow. Or you can try tossing in a small piece of bread or biscuit just out of reach. Never frighten the dog and never throw him in. Once he starts swimming be careful not to let him do too much. He will be using different muscles and may become tired quite quickly. Also be careful at the sea. A rough sea and a strong tide can be too much for the best of swimmers.

Jumping

Be careful not to start a puppy jumping before he is about six to nine months old. Too much jumping before the pup is properly grown can cause all sorts of troubles, including deformities. To start with be careful that you only ask him to jump a low, solid object. That way he won't hurt himself and will gain confidence. Put up a small jump in the garden. Next to the fence is a good idea as it helps to stop him running out. Put him on a leash, climb over yourself and giving a sharp tug call him after you. Once he understands the command run up to the jump with him and let out the leash so that he goes over on his own. Have him jumping freely on command over the small jump before you raise it. And if he starts running out, put the leash back on. As with swimming, dogs that like retrieving will usually learn quickly if an object is thrown over the jump for them to fetch.

Always keep the dog on the leash until he will jump over the hurdle reliably on a word of command only.

Before you say, 'I don't think I want to teach my dog to jump', just think of the advantages to you and the dog. Imagine a country walk with a large, hairy and very muddy Old English Sheepdog: you come to a style, and the dog won't jump! It is not much fun trying to heave that sort of parcel over a style or fence. It will make walks so much more fun for the dog and interesting for you. There will be fallen trees, ditches, banks, stone walls, all sorts of natural hazards for the dog to try. Not only will he enjoy it and benefit from the extra exercise, it also teaches him obedience. Make him sit and wait until you tell him to jump, call him back again. Throw something for him to fetch. All of which will exercise his mind as well as his body. Avoid barbed wire fences, spiked palings and any fence with loose wires in which the dog might become entangled.

Smaller dogs, obviously, cannot tackle big jumps, but they too can have great fun with small ones. Teach them to jump over a walking stick, over your leg, through your arms.

Once the dog has been taught to jump, on his own, over a small jump put him back on the leash, hold a stick in front of him and give him the command to jump. Once he does this, take the leash off and gradually increase the height of the stick from the ground. After that, it is easy to get him to jump over your leg. Raise your leg out in front of you, hold the stick along it and tell him to jump. After a few times it should be possible to remove the stick and just have him jump over your leg.

It is best to teach a dog to jump through a hoop before you teach him to jump through your arms. Use a fairly large hoop at first. A good one can be made from a piece of garden hose and it won't hurt the dog if he knocks it. Have him on the leash, hold the hoop, low to the ground in front of him and have the leash

Once your dog jumps happily over a stick try him over your leg. Start by holding the stick out with the leg, as shown here.

Once the dog has learnt to jump through a hoop, he should easily learn to jump through your arms. First wrap your arms right round the hoop like this. If he jumps through that, take away the hoop and just make a circle with your arms.

through the hoop. Give him a command to jump through, (make it different from the one you use to jump over or you will muddle him), at the same time give a small jerk on the leash and encourage him with your voice. As soon as he gets the hang of it, take the leash off and increase the height at which you hold the hoop. To get him to jump through your arms simply circle your arms round the hoop and with any luck he will jump straight through. If he doesn't like the idea, you will need a helper to hold the hoop in that way, while you jump him through on the leash, but this is seldom necessary. As with the stick and your leg, discard the hoop as soon as you can and just jump him through your arms.

Some people have an aversion to teaching dogs to do tricks. But the one thing a dog does not want to do is nothing! To him anything is better than that. And tricks are often more fun for both dog and trainer than negative obedience exercises. The more fun that can be put into training, the stronger will be the bond between dog and trainer.

Dogs in the country

Most people enjoy a day out in the country, taking along the family dog. And someone will probably say, 'Ben will have a lovely time chasing rabbits over the downs'. But if Ben is a 'townie' he won't be used to the countryside and the livestock found there. In Britain the law, often very loosely interpreted, says that any dog found worrying livestock may be shot, if it cannot be stopped any other way. In some other countries any dog seen near livestock is shot on sight. Ben, chasing after a rabbit, may suddenly find himself in the middle of a flock of sheep. The sheep will panic and if in lamb, many will abort. Apart from that, the excited dog will then chase the sheep instead of the rabbit, which by now will be well away. So many more sheep will be injured or killed. The fact that you are quite sure 'he was only playing and didn't mean any harm' won't help the sheep, the farmer or the dog.

So before you decide to let your dog enjoy his free gallop, be quite sure that he is obedient and will come back when called. Never let him run out of your sight, and make sure there are no livestock around, even in the distance. Remember that just as he instinctively chased a ball as a puppy, so he is likely to chase anything that runs whether it is sheep, cattle or anything else. If you stop to have a picnic, tie him up in a shady spot and then you can all relax and enjoy yourselves.

You might also meet cattle, most of which are inquisitive creatures and will often come charging across a field if they see a strange dog. Cattle, especially cows with calves, are quite capable of doing serious damage to a dog. A dog wandering up to a small calf lying in long grass will be lucky to escape with his life if the cow comes up to protect her offspring. So never take your dog into a field of cows and calves, not even if he is on a leash.

If the footpath takes you through a field of cattle without calves, it should be quite safe if the dog is on a leash. If the cattle do come over to have a look at you keep the dog quiet and just walk on calmly. Don't start shouting and shooing at them. It will only excite the dog and he may start barking and cause general chaos.

You are also likely to meet horseriders on bridleways and grassy tracks. Most country horses are used to dogs and take little notice of them under normal circumstances. But not all dogs are used to horses, so be careful. Horses are very easily startled and a dog suddenly rushing out of the bushes could cause a horse to shy or even bolt, resulting in a nasty accident. So if riders are about and you are not too sure of your dog, keep him on the leash. If he is sensible and under control, call him back to you if you see a rider approaching. Then make him lie down quietly until the rider has passed.

Useful addresses

Great Britain

Animal Health Trust, 24 Portland Place, London W1N 4HN

Blue Cross (Animal Hospital), 1 Hugh Street, London SW1V 1QQ

British Union for the Abolition of Vivisection (pet home-finding service), 47 Whitehall, London SW1A 2BZ

British Veterinary Association, 7 Mansfield Street, London W1M 0AT

Canine Press Ltd, 7 Greenwich South Street, London SE10 8BR

Central Dog Registry Ltd, 49 Marloes Road, London W8 6LA

The Dogs' Home, 4 Battersea Park Road, London SW8 4AA.

Dog World (weekly show paper), 32 New Street, Ashford, Kent TN23 1QW

Anthony Green & Co. (Pets Bazaar—pet accessory mail order service), Kilburn Place, London NW6 1YD

International Society for the Protection of Animals, 106 Jermyn Street, London SW1Y 6EE

Kennel Club, 1 Clarges Street, Piccadilly, London W1Y 8AB

Ministry of Agriculture, Fisheries and Food (Animal Exports and Imports), Animal Health Division, Government Buildings, Hook Rise South, Surbiton, Surry KT6 7NF

National Anti-Vivisection Society Ltd (pet home-finding service), 51 Harley Street, London W1N 1DD

National Canine Defence League, 10 Seymour Street, London W1H 1DD

National Dog Owners' Association, 92 High Street, Lee-on-Solent, Hampshire PO13 9BU

National Pets Club, *Daily Mirror*, 33 Holborn, London EC1P 1DQ

Our Dogs (weekly show paper), Oxford Road, Station Approach, Manchester M60 1SX

Pro-Dogs Organization, Arden House, Holt Wood, Aylesford, Kent

People's Dispensary for Sick Animals, PDSA House, South Street, Dorking, Surrey RH4 2LB

Pedigree Education Centre, Stanhope House, Stanhope Place, London W2 2HH

Pets' Welcome Holiday Guide, 23a Brighton Road, South Croydon, Surrey CR2 6UE

Retired Greyhound Trust, St Martins House, 140 Tottenham Court Road, London W1P 0AS

Royal Society for the Prevention of Cruelty to Animals, The Manor House, Horsham, Sussex RH12 1HG

USA

American Society for the Prevention of Cruelty to Animals
  (ASPCA), 441 E 92nd Street, New York, NY 10028
National Dog Registry, 227 Stebbins Road, Carmel, NY 10512
Animal Medical Center, 510 E 62nd Street, New York, NY 10023
American Kennel Club, 51 Madison Avenue, New York, NY 10010

Canada

Canadian Council on Animal Care, 151 Slater Street, Ottawa,
  Ontario K1P 5H3
Canadian Federation of Humane Societies, 900 Pinecrest Road,
  Ottawa, Ontario K2B 6B3
Canadian Kennel Club, 2150 Bloor Street West, Toronto, Ontario

Australia

Canine Association of Western Australia, P.O. Box 135, Claremont,
  Western Australia 6010
Kennel Association of Queensland, Sturgeon Street, Ormiston,
  Queensland 4163
North Australian Canine Association, 9 Brogan Street, Darwin,
  Northern Territory 5790
South Australian Canine Association Inc., Showgrounds, Wayville,
  South Australia 5034

South Africa

The Kennel Union of South Africa, P.O. Box 562, Cape Town 8000

NB Many specialist breed societies operate rescue services for
members of their breed and assist in home finding. Addresses of
breed clubs can be obtained from the Kennel Club or the canine
press.

Index

Page numbers in *italic* refer to illustrations.

Afghan Hound 17, 71
anal sacs 75
artificial respiration 81
association of ideas 10–11, *10*, 24,
    25

barking, in empty house 33–4
    parked car 33
baskets 76
bathing 75–6
bean bags 76
bedding 76
beds, 35, 76
begging 84–5, *85*
behaviour of the mother 24–5
being left alone 33–4
bleeding 83
boarding kennels 79
brushes 71
burns 81

car sickness 31–2
castration 14–15, 39
catching 85
Chihuahuas 22, 70
choking 83
choosing the right dog 18–20
Chows 72
clipping 72
collars *43*, 44–5, *44*, *45*
    flea 71
combs 71
commercial diet 77
convalescence 80–1
correction 11, *50*
correction and reward 24–5, 27

Dachshunds 22

dew claws 74
diarrhoea 81
distemper 23, 79
dog guard 32
dogs and babies 41–2
    cattle 88–9
    countryside 88–9
    horses 89
    other pets 40–1, *40*
    poultry 16
    sheep 16, 88
down 51–4, *51*, *53*
drop on command 53–4
drowning 81
dry food 77
dying for his country 85

ears 73–4, *73*
Elizabethan collar 80, *81*
emergency muzzle 82–3, *82*
eyes 72

feeding 76–7
feed bowls, aluminium 22
    earthenware 22
    stainless steel 22
feet 74
fleas 71
fighting 37–9
first aid 81–3

general care 70–7
German Shepherd Dog 46
going on a leash 29–30, *30*
Greyhound 17
grooming 70–5, *70*, *71*, 80
gums 73
guarding 64–9, *67*

gun dog 16, *16*, 77
gun shyness 18

hardpad 79
health 78–81
heart worms 78
heat stroke 82
heelwork 44–8, *46*
heel free 47
hepatitis 23
hookworms 78
hounds 17
hound glove 71
housetraining 24, 26–8

instincts 11–18, *16*, 25
   guarding 13, 58, 64–5, 68
   hunting 12, 13, 15–16, 58, 59, 63, 68
   maternal 12
   pack 13, 37
   retrieving 12, 58, 59
   self-preservation 13, 14
   sex 13, 14
   to keep nest clean 13, 26–8
intelligence 11, 12

jumping 87–8, *87–8*
jumping up 36–7, *37*

Keeshonds 72
kennels 22
   indoor 22
   outdoor 35

learning his name 25–6
leashes 45
   harness 30
   spring-loaded 30
leptospirosis 23, 79
lice 71–2

medicine, administration of 80, *80*
minerals 77

nails 74
   clipping 74, *74*
nervousness 14
nose 73

nursing 79–81

Old English Sheepdog 71
operations 80
   see also convalescence

pack leader 17
parvo virus 23, 79
Pekingese 71
pet insurance policy 24
pills, administration of 79, *79*
playpen 21, 22, *22*, 27
play and exercise 84–9
pointer *16*
poisoning 81–2
Pomeranians 72
Poodles 70, 72
puppies 21–8
   arrival 21–4
   bedding 21
   beds 21
   collars 22, 29
   correcting over-aggression 68–9, *69*
   feeding 23, 76
   grooming 22
   leashes 22, 29
   preparation for 21–4

rabies 23, 79
recall to handler 54–6
retrieving 58–64
   forcing method 58, 59–62, *60–2*
   natural 58–9
reward 11
roundworms 78
running wire 35, *35*

St Bernard 70
seek back 63–4, *64*
shaking hands 84, *84*
shampoo 75
   medicated 71, 75
sheath 74
sheepdog 16, *16*, 17
sit and stay 50–1
sit at the halt 48–50, *49*
spaying 14–15
speaking 86

stand 46–7, *56*
stomach worms 78
stripping 72
submissiveness 16, 17
swimming 86

tapeworms 78
teeth 73
   scaling 73, *73*
temperament 18–20
temperature 80, *80*
terriers 17, 72
tetanus 79
ticks 71
toys 23
traffic accidents 82–3, *83*

training, applied 58–69
   basic 29–42
   car 31–2
   obedience 43–57
training classes 43
tricks 84–6
tying up 34–6

vaccinations 23, 78–9
vitamins 77
vomiting 81, 82

whip worms 78
Whippet 46
Wire Fox Terriers 72
worming 20, 23, 78